DATE DUE

Creative
Problem
Solving

Recent Titles from Quorum Books

CREATIVE PROBLEM SOLVING

A Guide for
Trainers and Management

Arthur B. VanGundy

Q QUORUM BOOKS
NEW YORK
WESTPORT, CONNECTICUT
LONDON

Library of Congress Cataloging-in-Publication Data

VanGundy, Arthur B.
  Creative problem solving.

  Bibliography: p.
  Includes index.
  1. Problem solving.   2. Creative ability in business.
I. Title.
HD30.29.V34   1987   153.4′3   86–20484
ISBN 0–89930–170–3 (lib. bdg. : alk. paper)

Library of Congress Catalog Card Number: 86–20484
ISBN: 0–89930–170–3

First published in 1987 by Quorum Books

Greenwood Press, Inc.
88 Post Road West, Westport, Connecticut 06881

Printed in the United States of America

The paper used in this book complies with the
Permanent Paper Standard issued by the National
Information Standards Organization (Z39.48–1984).

10 9 8 7 6 5 4 3 2 1

To
Sidney J. Parnes,
who inspired me to become
a more creative problem solver.

Contents

Figures

Creative
Problem
Solving

1
Introduction to Creative Problem Solving

Most people have their own views about problem solving. You probably are no different. You may believe, for example, that good problem solvers are born and not made, that problems can be dealt with by systematically applying rational and analytical thinking, and that problem solving is simply a matter of locating the "correct" solution. On the other hand, you may believe that problem solving is a skill that can be learned, that intuition plays a major role in successful problem solving, and that many problems can be resolved with a number of different solutions.

Although you may believe in one or the other of these two schools of thought, you probably see some validity in aspects of both. You are born with certain attributes that can affect your ability to deal with problems. However, there also are certain problem solving skills that you acquire throughout your life. Rational and analytical thought are important to problem solving, but so is intuitive thinking. In fact, it is difficult to avoid using either, given the way our brains function. It is likely, however, that some types of problems may require more of one type of thinking than another. Finally you probably believe that some situations require one "correct" solution, while others may have many different "correct" solutions.

What is known as the Osborn-Parnes Creative Problem Solving (CPS) model (Osborn, 1963; Parnes, 1967; Parnes, Noller & Biondi, 1977; Isaksen & Treffinger, 1985) incorporates both schools of thought. It assumes that you possess both innate and acquired abilities, that both analytical and intuitive thinking are needed within different stages of the process, and that solution "correctness" is a matter of choice, arising from consideration of many possible solutions.

The CPS process is not a panacea for all of your problems, but it can help you deal with many difficult situations. In particular, CPS will be especially useful when you are faced with relatively ill-structured, ambiguous problem "messes" for which no ready-made solutions are available. For instance, a downturn in productivity, employee dissatisfaction, difficulties with unions, employee absenteeism, and stagnant product development all are examples of situations that might be dealt with using CPS.

Unfortunately, the term "creative problem solving" frequently is misleading. To many people, the word "creative" implies something magical or even something slightly tainted—suggesting more than actually can be offered. For example, we are bombarded every day with advertisements for workshops and publications dealing with creative financing, creative selling, creative cooking, creative carpentry, creative marketing, and so on. The list is almost endless. What usually is meant by "creative" in these ads is that they offer a different or better approach. Unfortunately, for the unwary consumer, "different" and "better" do not always equate with "creative." "Different" and "better" often amount to no more than a lot of "creative" exaggerated claims.

In the CPS approach, the word "creative" helps distinguish CPS from other problem solving models. In these other models, the emphasis usually is more upon analytical thinking. As mentioned, CPS involves both creative and analytical types of thinking, but the emphasis is somewhat more upon the creative. This emphasis is due largely to the types of problems for which the approach is most appropriate. The CPS model also is creative in the sense that it can help you find new ways of dealing with problems for which you have no prior experience. Thus, the CPS model is not represented as a "new and improved" approach to problem solving. Instead, you should view it as one approach that might be appropriate for many types of problems—especially those that are new to you.

PROBLEM TYPES

As already noted, CPS is most appropriate for ambiguous, ill-structured types of problems. Chances are that you probably haven't thought of classifying most of your problems in such a way. However, minimal familiarity with problem types can help in understanding how useful CPS can be. Furthermore, a basic knowledge of the structure of problems can make it easier to deal with a greater variety of problems.

There are many different ways to classify problems. One that has been used frequently in the problem solving literature is to describe problems as being well-structured, ill-structured, or semi-structured (e.g., Simon, 1973; MacCrimmon & Taylor, 1976).

In general, well-structured problems are relatively clear-cut and can be resolved using ready-made, routine solutions. For example, assembling a bicycle might be a well-structured problem because all you have to do is follow the instructions (this will not always be the case on Christmas Eve!).

An ill-structured problem, in contrast, must be dealt with using custom-made, nonroutine solutions. For these types of problems, you must invent a solution and hope that it will be successful. By comparison, ready-made solutions almost always will guarantee success for well-structured problems.

Situations that fall between well-structured and ill-structured problems possess elements of both. Generally known as semi-structured problems, these problems can be resolved using custom-made solutions, ready-made solutions, or elements of both.

Of these three problem types, ill-structured problems usually will be the most difficult to resolve. Because of the uncertainty involved and the need to design a custom solution, you will need to spend the most time dealing with these problems. Because of this, you will want to use the most efficient and effective method possible. That's where the CPS model comes in handy. With CPS, you not only can use your time economically, but also increase the odds of achieving a workable solution.

When you deal with different types of problems, you should be aware that your perceptions of these situations are subjective. Other people may see them in an entirely different light. What you see as semi-structured, for example, someone else might see as ill-structured or well-structured. The Christmas Eve bicycle assembly task could be well-structured for someone experienced with similar tasks, but ill-structured for someone who has never assembled anything mechanical. Thus, the existence of problem types is a relative, subjective phenomenon.

The manner in which you classify a problem will depend upon your overall familiarity with the major components of the problem (Taylor, 1974). Familiarity with a problem can be determined by evaluating how much you know about three problem components: an initial state, a goal state, and the transformations needed to make the initial state more like the goal state (Reitman, 1964, 1965). When dealing with a well-structured problem, you are familiar with all three components. In contrast, you are not familiar with the components of an ill-structured problem. To resolve these types of problems, you need to increase your familiarity.

Increasing problem familiarity is the basic process involved in using the CPS model (VanGundy, 1986). For instance, you might begin with a semi-structured situation in which you are familiar with the initial state, relatively unfamiliar with the goal state, and only vaguely familiar with possible transformations. As you acquire more information about the components, the situation eventually should evolve into a well-structured problem. At that point, a workable solution should emerge.

To illustrate this process, consider the problem of improving a product such as a food storage bag. For someone in the industry, the components of this problem might be perceived as follows. The initial state should be

relatively familiar. You probably understand the technology behind manufacturing of the bag, the basic chemistry involved in producing it, how it
works, and a few problems encountered in manufacturing or consumer use.
The goal state, in contrast, would be unfamiliar if you are dissatisfied with
the initial state or simply desire to make some improvements. Unless there
is a specific improvement you have in mind, you would need to gather
additional information to help you decide what particular goal state you
would like. For instance, you might want to decide upon changes in closure
methods, storage capabilities, or air retention properties. Because of your
uncertainty about the goal state, you would not be able to suggest a potential
transformation until the goal state is resolved. However, even if you decide
upon a goal state, you still might be uncertain about possible transformations. There may be several ways to alter the closure method, for example.
In any event, you would need to generate several potential transformations
and select the best one.

A BRIEF HISTORY OF CPS

The scientific study of creative problem solving has its roots in the work
of numerous social scientists. Most of the early research focused upon the
creative personality (e.g., Guilford, 1950, 1959; MacKinnon, 1962, 1965)
and creative thinking abilities (e.g., Torrance, 1962, 1963). Two major
outcomes of this research were Guilford's "Structure of the Intellect" model
(Guilford, 1959) and the Torrance Tests of Creative Thinking (Torrance,
1974).

The CPS model itself, however, arose directly out of the work of Alex
F. Osborn (1953), now regarded as the "father of brainstorming." As an
advertising executive, Osborn had a long-term interest in creativity and
problem solving. He wrote extensively on the topics and was a major
influence on the field of CPS.

According to Osborn, creative thinking involves three basic stages: fact-
finding, idea-finding, and solution-finding. Fact-finding is concerned with
two substages: problem definition and preparation. The purpose of problem
definition is to define problems by breaking them down into their major
parts. Preparation is intended to help problem understanding by collecting
relevant problem information. Osborn's idea-finding stage was used to
generate potential ideas and then refine them to be as workable as possible.
Solution-finding, the third stage, is used to evaluate the ideas and select
those with the highest potential for problem resolution.

In addition to his three-stage model, another important contribution of
Osborn was his development of brainstorming principles. The first principle
stated that idea generation should be separated from idea evaluation. He
called this the principle of deferred judgment. Our tendency to judge ideas
must be suppressed to allow our creative sides to express themselves. The

second principle stated that quantity breeds quality. That is, the greater the number of ideas you generate, the greater the possibility that a high-quality solution (i.e., one capable of resolving the problem) will be produced.

In 1949, Osborn began teaching a course in creative thinking at the University of Buffalo in Buffalo, New York. He also founded the Creative Education Foundation in Buffalo in 1954 and helped start the annual Creative Problem Solving Institutes (CPSI) in 1955. These institutes have been held every year since and often draw 500 or more participants from the United States and several foreign countries.

Psychologist Sidney J. Parnes (1967) was influenced by Osborn's work and recognized its potential for creative problem solving. Parnes initially made two major improvements upon Osborn's model, later added several refinements, conducted an extensive research program along with his associates, and continues to contribute to the model's development today. Now a Professor Emeritus at the Center for Studies in Creativity at the State University College at Buffalo, Parnes continues to play an active role in the annual institutes and the field of creative problem solving in general.

Parnes' initial contribution to Osborn's work was to extend Osborn's three-stage model to five. Parnes inserted a problem-finding stage between the fact-finding and idea-finding stages and an acceptance-finding stage following the solution-finding stage. With these additions, greater emphasis was placed upon developing an understanding of the problem and making provisions for solution implementation.

Parnes recognized the importance of taking the time to explore alternative problem redefinitions before settling on one definition and generating ideas. As you no doubt have experienced, we sometimes generate a lot of ideas for the "wrong" problem. Thus, addition of a separate stage for problem-finding seemed to be justified. Parnes' addition of the acceptance-finding stage arose out of the importance of solution implementation. Selection of the best solution in the world for your problem will be a fruitless exercise unless you can develop an action plan and get it implemented.

Another major contribution of Parnes was his recognition of the convergent and divergent activities involved in each stage of the model. Although many people think of creativity solely in terms of divergent activities (i.e., generating many different ideas), CPS actually involves much more.

Problem solving in each stage of the model begins with a divergent search for whatever is required within the stage. Thus, the problem solver begins fact-finding, problem-finding, idea-finding, solution-finding, and acceptance-finding by searching, respectively, for relevant facts, more broadened alternative problem definitions, potential solutions, evaluation criteria and workable solutions, and ways to implement the selected solution. The convergent activities within each stage of Parnes' original five-stage model involve selecting (or converging upon): relevant facts (fact-finding), the best redefinition of the original problem "mess" (problem-finding), the ideas with the highest potential for resolving the problem (idea-finding), the best selection criteria and the most workable solutions (solution-finding), and the most important actions needed to implement the chosen solution.

In Parnes' original model, the problem solver begins with awareness about some ambiguous challenge, concern, or opportunity. Next, he or she identifies and analyzes the general problem "mess" and selects a target area to focus upon. The problem solver then enters the fact-finding stage and proceeds through the model until actions are taken to resolve the problem and new challenges are presented. At this point, the process might begin again or start from any one of the stages.

RESEARCH ON THE CPS MODEL

Since its development, numerous studies have been conducted on the effectiveness of the CPS model alone (e.g., Parnes & Brunelle, 1967; Parnes & Noller, 1972a, 1972b) and in comparison with other approaches (e.g., Torrance, 1972; Mansfield, Busse & Krepelka, 1978). Results of these studies have been somewhat mixed and will not be reviewed here.

However, some of the confusion about the effectiveness of creativity training may be due to an overreliance upon the number of statistically significant results obtained. According to Rose and Lin (1984), the magnitude of the effects of training programs cannot be assessed using conventional inferential statistics. Instead, something known as a "meta-analysis" is required. Using this type of analysis, Rose and Lin evaluated the results of 46 research studies. Each of these studies used Torrance's Tests of Creative Thinking (Torrance, 1974) to measure the variables of fluency, flexibility, originality, and elaboration.

The Osborn-Parnes CPS model was compared with results of the Productive Thinking Program (Covington & Crutchfield, 1965; Covington, Crutchfield, Davies & Olton, 1974), the Purdue Creative Thinking Program (Feldhusen, Speedie & Treffinger, 1971), and a variety of other studies that combined different training techniques. Overall, creativity training accounted for 22 percent of the variance in the creative performance of the study participants (or, approximately 78 percent of their performance was due to factors other than the training).

However, there was considerable variability in the effects of training upon different types of creative performance and across the different training programs. Of special note was the finding that training using the Osborn-Parnes model produced the highest impact on the creative outcome measures (verbal originality was affected most by the CPS training). Rose and Lin concluded their study by observing: "The substantial impact of Osborn and Parnes CPS on verbal creativity combined with the conclusions from both Torrance's and Parnes' and Brunelle's reviews provide strong evidence to support the effectiveness of this program. The use of CPS in education and business should foster more original thinking among practitioners" (Rose & Lin, 1984, p. 21).

SOME CAUTIONS AND PROMISES

Although more research clearly is needed to further assess the validity of the CPS model, it appears to be a useful program for improving creative problem solving performance. Given its fairly widespread use and flexibility of application, CPS appears to be an ideal model for training others as well as helping solve problems in general.

In learning about this model and practicing with it, you should be aware of its limitations as well as its more promising features. No model, in any field, can claim to be perfect for all situations and all people.

As already noted, the model is not necessarily appropriate for dealing with all types of problems. The most appropriate situations will be those for which you must create new solutions.

Second, there will be many situations in which the entire model will not be needed. Of the six steps involved in the model to be described, you may need to use only one or two for some situations, while five or six may seem more appropriate for other challenges facing you. You will have to be the judge, since how much you use the model will depend upon how well you initially understand the challenges and concerns you perceive. For example, I currently am working with a large corporation in the area of corporate planning. They are looking for some fresh perspectives to use in long-range planning. At this time, they believe they have isolated the major challenges they face. As a result, I suggest we start working with the second step of the model, fact-finding.

Third, the model is presented in a linear, sequential manner. However, you may not want to use it this way for dealing with many problems. Because information about your problems often changes over time, you may find yourself returning to a previous stage or jumping ahead to a new stage. Again, the decision to deviate from the linear aspect of the model entirely depends upon your perceptions about your problem.

Finally, this model may not be for everyone. To learn about this model, you must be motivated to improve your problem solving abilities. Otherwise, it will be just another useless tool to lay aside for future reference. As has been documented in the research literature, internal motivation is a prime determinant of creative performance (Amabile, 1983).

So much for the cautions. Now the promise.

The most significant promise of the CPS model is that it can awaken the creative genius within you. Whether you like it or not, you are a creative individual. And you have the capacity to become even more creative. All it takes is a little motivation and some structure to facilitate your learning.

Because of the way the CPS model is organized, practicing with it should help you internalize many basic creative thinking principles and help you overcome obstacles that prevent you from becoming more creative. Thus, you might view this book as more than a resource for helping you deal with problems. You also might view it as an opportunity to improve your creative problem solving abilities. Ideally, you will integrate the learnings of the model into your own problem solving repertoire. Then you can apply the important features of the model in a natural manner and with little conscious effort.

ADVANTAGES OF CPS: WHO NEEDS IT?

You may not be concerned with awakening the "creative genius" sleeping inside of you and becoming a more creative person. Instead, you might be more concerned with solving the day-to-day problems you encounter in your work. If so, then CPS can help you do this and benefit your organization in many other ways as well. The following list of advantages (many of which are interrelated) is by no means exhaustive. However, it should provide you with a basic understanding of some of the benefits of training people in CPS and using it on a regular basis.

1. CPS can help you uncover unexplored opportunity areas in your personal life as well as in your organization. In your personal life, CPS can help you explore career goals, for example. Or it can help you resolve and deal with any number of interpersonal problems. In organizations, CPS can illuminate potential business development opportunities and open up new ways for better using human and material resources.

2. By exploring new opportunity areas more efficiently and effectively, an organization should be able to increase its competitive advantage. Not only will a systematic approach to problem solving make you more efficient, it also should result in higher-quality solutions.

3. CPS can help individuals and organizations increase their freedom of choice. By providing a greater number of options from which to choose, you will maximize the possibility of successfully resolving your problems.

4. Many people have the need to exert more control over their lives instead of allowing chance or outside forces to be in control. Using CPS for planning and dealing with major problems can give you greater control over your life's events. You can take charge of your problems rather than allowing them to be in charge of you. Clearly, organizations that can control their future directions (as much as the future can be controlled) will place themselves in a more competitive position.

5. Because CPS is a generic problem solving model, it will be useful for dealing with a variety of ill-structured problems. Some of these problems exist now, but you undoubtedly will encounter others in the future. As a result of its flexibility, the CPS model will allow you to approach both current and future problems more confidently. Problems you cannot an-

ticipate now should not worry you if you know you have the skills to apply a flexible problem solving approach.

6. We often become bogged down in the routines of our daily lives. CPS can help us open up and explore exciting new possibilities and challenges. If you do not think you need any more "excitement" in your life, then CPS can help you deal better with new situations.

7. CPS can help you discover new talents and insights about yourself. Like everyone else, you are in a constant state of growth and change. CPS can help you to gain a better perspective on this growth and determine how your efforts might be best channeled. This is especially important in large organizations where human resources are not always fully used.

8. All of us are both creative and analytical. Our brains are organized in such a way that we need to use judgment as well as intuitive thinking. Because CPS emphasizes both creative and analytical thinking, it can help you use these types of thinking more harmoniously. That is, the CPS process can enable you to target your thinking capabilities more effectively for resolving problems.

9. Time often is an important element in the resolution of any problem. Delaying action can lead to disasterous consequences. With the CPS model, it usually is possible to shorten the time between initial problem perception and its eventual solution. The systematic and relatively structured elements of CPS make it easy to target your efforts and keep on track until you reach a workable solution.

10. In organizations, CPS frequently is used in group settings. One outcome can be an improvement in communication among employees. Being together in a face-to-face situation can force people to communicate more frequently and openly. Other related advantages are possible increases in the ability to express one's self and enhancement of listening skills—both made possible by working together in groups.

11. Group use of CPS also can help you better appreciate the capabilities of others in the organization and the resources they can contribute when solving problems. When we deal with most of our problems as individuals, we don't have the opportunity to benefit from the contributions of others. Group CPS removes people from routine problem solving situations and allows them to experience creative thinking. However, care must be exercised in regard to this advantage. Not all people in an organization want or should be presented with creative problem solving opportunities. Much organizational work is routine and should be in order to maintain efficiency.

12. Most ill-structured, ambiguous organizational problems are accompanied by varying degrees of uncertainty and stress (McCaskey, 1982). When these levels exceed optimal amounts, performance can decrease. CPS, however, can help reduce problem solving stress and uncertainty. As noted, knowing you can use a flexible model for dealing with ill-structured problems should increase your problem solving confidence. If you are confident

about your abilities, then you should experience less dysfunctional uncertainty and stress.

13. In general, CPS can help organizations benefit in such areas as engineering, R & D, new product development, strategic planning, marketing and advertising, and basic management problems involving people and other resources.

FUTURE OF CPS AND RECOMMENDATIONS

Predicting the future obviously is a risky business. Like everyone else, I am not equipped to predict anything except death and taxes (e.g., "you'll pay your taxes, then you'll die") with any high degree of certainty. Nevertheless, I would like to attempt a few predictions about the CPS model. Because it is easier to predict what should happen than what will happen, I also have made some recommendations about future directions. These predictions and recommendations are based primarily upon my own subjective perceptions and insights about the model. The following are presented in no particular order.

1. As CPS becomes more widely known and practiced, business will make greater use of the model in its training programs. CPS should be especially attractive during difficult economic times and when competition is high.

2. Scholars will continue to refine and elaborate upon the basic framework of the model. However, the current framework will not be altered drastically. The changes either will be minor or a new framework will be conceptualized and developed.

3. A greater number of techniques will be developed or modified to use within the different stages. Except in idea-finding where there is an abundance of available techniques, more techniques could be used to facilitate the other stages. The recent contributions of Isaksen and Treffinger (1985) in this area are noteworthy. However, caution must be exercised so that users do not become oversaturated with techniques. Techniques should not become an end in themselves.

4. Software programs for CPS are clearly needed. Given the increasing sophistication and complexity of the model, user resistance is likely to increase unless the model can become more "user friendly." Somewhat ironically, computer technology has the potential to make CPS more accessible and acceptable to greater numbers of users.

5. There will be a slightly greater awareness of the importance of the first three steps of the model. Understanding the problem situation is essential for successful problem resolution. In one respect, it probably is more important to be successful at analyzing and selecting problems than to be proficient at idea generation.

6. More systematic approaches are needed for choosing from among

techniques. Due to the number of techniques available, the user is faced with a baffling assortment of methods. The author currently is working on conceptualizing this problem. However, empirical research is greatly needed.

7. More flexible applications of the model are needed. Many first time users may worry needlessly about applying the model "just right" and using all of the stages in the correct sequence. As Parnes and many others have noted, the model was designed to be used flexibly. Not all stages will be needed in all situations. There also is nothing wrong with recycling your problem solving efforts. As new information becomes available about a situation, you may need to return to an earlier stage in the model.

8. In general, much more research is needed on the effectiveness of the model in a variety of situations. Moreover, multiple evaluation criteria (i.e., dependent variables) are needed to validate the model's usefulness and applicability further.

SUGGESTIONS FOR TRAINERS

The way you introduce the CPS model can be almost as important as how you teach people to use it. The initial reactions people have to the model will shape their attitudes and expectations. If people don't have positive attitudes at the outset, their experiences in using the model may be negative. As a result, you probably will want to spend some time deciding upon the best approach to use when introducing the model.

The following suggestions for introducing CPS might help you in planning your approach. However, you undoubtedly will want to tailor your design to best fit the needs of the people you train. The suggestions are presented according to the subheadings used in the chapter. There is nothing special about the order of presentation, except for the need to focus some attention at the outset upon dealing with expectations. Other than that, you probably will want to pick and choose from among the suggestions. Moreover, you may want to include some material from the chapters dealing with obstacles to creativity (Chapter 2) and creative thinking principles and exercises (Chapters 3 and 4).

General introduction. After presenting an overview of the program and the mechanics of where and when you will meet, ask the participants about their general expectations. For example, you might ask them how they feel about participating, why they are participating, what they hope to get out of the program, and what they think are the positive and negative results of participation in problem solving training.

Next, you might generally discuss the topics of creativity and problem solving. Point out that everyone is creative, but we usually fail to live up to our creative potential. However, we can be trained to become more creative. When dealing with a skeptical audience, I sometimes note that I approach creativity from a problem solving perspective. Most people seem better able to relate to problem solving than creativity. You also could mention that the program will focus upon special types of problems. Then, give a few general examples.

Finish up your initial remarks by asking for questions and perhaps summarizing points you and the group members have made so far. Then, tell the group what you will do next.

Because we all approach problems differently, you might want to devote some time to the topic of learning style differences. The "hands-on" instruments available for this topic also can help motivate the participants and increase their interest level in the program.

A considerable body of literature exists on how we all think and learn differently. As a result, our approaches to problems will differ also. Being aware of our personal learning styles can help us understand better how we approach problems and, perhaps, how we should approach problems. A variety of instruments exists for assessing learning styles, but only two will be mentioned here.

One widely known instrument is the Learning Style Inventory (Kolb, Rubin & McIntyre, 1974). The authors hypothesize that learning involves a four-stage cycle: a concrete experience, observing and reflecting upon the concrete experience, developing abstractions and generalizations, and forming new hypotheses to test using new experiences. The instrument itself is designed to measure the perceived importance to individuals of each of these stages. The four measures used correspond to the four stages of the authors' model: concrete experience (CE), reflective observation (RO), abstract conceptualization (AC), and active experimentation (AE).

After completing the Learning Style Inventory, a score can be computed for each measure. These scores then can be plotted on a Learning Style Profile to show relative areas of importance. Scores also can be compared with others who have used this inventory.

Once the scores have been plotted, they can be used to form four basic style groups: accommodators (low AC-CE, high AE-RO), divergers (low AC-CE, low AE-RO), convergers (high AC-CE, high AE-RO), and assimilators (high AC-CE, low AE-RO). Each group is assumed to represent a different type of learning style. For more information on the Learning Style Inventory, you should consult the Kolb, Rubin, and McIntyre reference.

When using this inventory for training purposes, you might consider the following steps:

1. Have the participants complete and score the instrument and plot their scores on the Learning Style Profile.
2. Discuss the different learning styles.

3. Ask the group members to discuss how well their scores describe what they perceive to be their "real" learning styles (i.e., how they see themselves).

4. Ask the group members to discuss how the different learning styles might help them deal with different types of problems.

In addition to the Learning Style Inventory, another popular instrument is the Myers-Briggs Type Indicator (MBTI) (Myers, 1980). Like the Learning Style Inventory, the MBTI measures four preferences for learning styles. These areas are concerned with preferences for: working alone versus working with others to solve problems (extraversion-introversion), using your senses versus your personal insights in gathering information (sensing-intuition), making decisions based upon logical consequences and impersonal analysis as opposed to using personal values and considering what is important to you personally (thinking-feeling), and dealing with the world by evaluating it in a sequential and orderly manner or relying upon your senses and intuition (judging-perception). Different combinations of these types will determine your learning style. For example, you might score high on introversion, intuition, thinking, and judgment. If so, you probably are good at planning tasks, using independent thought to guide your behavior, somewhat skeptical, and often tenacious.

In discussing the MBTI, you can use essentially the same process described for the Learning Style Inventory. The only adjustments you'll need to make will be those required to conform to the specific format of each instrument.

Whichever instrument you use, be careful to note that most such instruments need to be used cautiously. Some instruments in this area are not designed as well as they might be. As a result, their primary value may be as rough indicators and not as absolute measures of learning styles. You should stress that these instruments provide data that we can consider and reflect upon. However, the results should be taken only at face value.

You might conclude your introductory section with a brief overview of the CPS process. However, instead of presenting the model and its different steps, guide the individual group members in working through an abbreviated version. That is, don't tell them what you are doing, just do it.

To do this, verbally provide major instructions for each stage. For example, you might start out by asking them to individually write down several challenges, concerns, or opportunities facing them now in their lives and to select one that is most important to them and can be worked on now (objective-finding). Have them state this problem using the IWWM format (in what ways might . . . ?). Next, have them write down all the relevant data they know concerning this problem and select areas that seem to be most important to them (fact-finding).

Continue this activity until you have gone through all six stages. When you are finished, ask the group if anyone believes he or she solved a problem or made some significant progress in dealing with one. Usually, a few people will report some degree of success. Then, ask them what they liked and disliked about the process, major problems they encountered, major areas of success, and so forth.

In using this abbreviated version, be sure to allow sufficient time to work through all six stages. If you go too fast, the experience may disillusion many of the participants and result in motivational problems later on. On the other hand, you don't want to spend too much time and ask them to do too much during this relatively brief encounter with the model. I find that I need at least 20 to 30 minutes for this activity.

Problem types. The major purpose of this section is to emphasize the variability that exists among problems. The math problems we dealt with in school, for example, are quite different from many types of management problems for which there might be more than one correct solution. Thus, a first point to stress would be that all problems are not alike.

You also might note that some problems are difficult to solve when we use an inappropriate problem solving language or approach (Adams, 1979). A general awareness of problem types can make it easier to determine the best approach to use. In particular, knowledge about problem types can lead to more appropriate use of the CPS model.

One way to introduce a discussion on problem types would be to present the group with a list of different problems (or, you could have the group generate its own list of problems). For instance, you might list such problems as: a car that doesn't start, employee dissatisfaction, encouraging more people to vote, and calculating a production rate. Then, ask the group to discuss which problems might be solved in more than one way. An outcome of this discussion might be classification of the problems on some sort of continuum between well-structured and ill-structured.

You also could examine the different degrees of ambiguity and uncertainty represented by each problem. This latter activity is especially important, since it should bring out differences in perception held by the group members (classifying the problems as well-structured or ill-structured will do the same thing). It is very important to stress that problem types are based upon individual perceptions and not upon any absolute classification scheme. Ownership is a vital consideration when dealing with any type of problem.

Some cautions and promises. For this section, you might consider using a soft-sell approach to the model. That is, you should avoid trying to force it upon anyone. Once people become familiar with CPS, they usually accept it on its merits. What you say is not likely to be as important as what can be gained from personal experience with CPS.

Of the material presented in the text, there are at least three major points you should make. First, note that the model is intended to be used flexibly.

You don't "have" to use all the stages for every problem and there is nothing wrong with recycling to previous stages. That is, people should feel free to move forward, backward, and "sideways" through the model. Second, using the model takes a certain amount of motivation to be successful. Like anything else, a "felt need" to change a situation is required. No one can be forced to solve problems and learn the model. Finally, point out that the process of learning the model and then practicing with it might help increase one's creative thinking ability. CPS is more than a technique. It is a learning process that can have some side benefits if a few fundamental concepts are integrated into one's problem solving behavior. The ultimate objective is to make people better problem solvers, not just learn how to use a model.

Advantages of CPS: Who needs it. In addition to the advantages listed in the text, you also might provide examples of situations that have benefited from CPS. For instance, I personally have been involved in such situations as: improving interoffice communications, generating product improvements, reducing paper work, and crystallizing organizational goals and objectives.

Perhaps the most important advantage of CPS is its ability to create new opportunities for individuals, groups, organizations, and societal institutions. CPS is more than another problem solving model. It is an opportunity generator that can open up entirely new avenues of exploration. Most of us respond more positively when we view a difficult situation as an opportunity and not as just another dreaded problem to be resolved. When viewed this way, the outcome usually will be more positive and acceptable.

A brief history of CPS. Unless your group is especially interested in the history behind the model, you might rely upon a brief lecture to discuss this material. In this lecture, you should note how the model evolved from Osborn's original model and how it continues to evolve.

Since you probably just finished having the group work through the model, this also would be a good time to discuss what they just did. When discussing the model, keep your comments fairly general. Don't try to include all of the finer points of the model. However, be sure to stress the divergent and convergent aspects of each stage and why they are important. Also, mention that all judgment must be withheld during all divergent activities.

Research on the CPS model. Unless your audience is research oriented and interested in validation studies, you might want to skip over this topic or treat it very lightly. One major point to emphasize is that the model has been scientifically compared to other creative thinking approaches and has emerged looking pretty good. However, like most areas of research, considerable study is needed before any definitive conclusions can be drawn.

Future of CPS and recommendations. As with the section on the history of CPS, you may want to devote relatively little time to the future of CPS. Although the future obviously is important and worthy of consideration, an introductory portion of a seminar probably is not an appropriate place to discuss it. However, if you think your class might be interested, initiate a discussion and ask for their predictions. Resist the temptation to judge these predictions. Too much of an expert role on your part could lead to unproductive negative attitudes on the part of the class.

Whatever you do during the introductory meetings, try to involve the class as much as possible. Their motivation is likely to increase and be sustained if they have a chance to participate. It is especially important that they be given a chance to experiment with the model and play with some creative thinking exercises (see Chapter 3 and 4, for example).

In addition to creating interest, your goal during the first one or two meetings should be to provide the class with a basic knowledge of the fundamental aspects of the model. Specifically, the participants should be able to: identify the six stages, describe the basic divergent and convergent activities within each stage, and be aware that the model is flexible and should be used flexibly.

SUMMARY

To be effective problem solvers, you need to use both analytical and intuitive types of thinking. The Osborn-Parnes Creative Problem Solving (CPS) model incorporates both types of thinking to help deal with problems for which there is more than one correct solution. In particular, the model is useful for dealing with ill-structured problems. These are problems for which you are relatively unfamiliar with the initial problem state, the goal state, or the transformations needed to make the initial state like the goal state.

The CPS model contains six stages: objective-finding, fact-finding, problem-finding, idea-finding, solution-finding, and acceptance-finding. Each stage involves divergent and convergent activities. For instance, in objective-finding, you diverge to identify problem "messes" facing you and then converge to select one you are motivated and able to deal with. The six stages will not be required in all situations and you may want to recycle to previous stages if you acquire new information during the problem solving process.

Among the advantages of the CPS model are: potential to uncover unexplored opportunity areas in your personal and work lives, increases in organizational competitiveness, flexibility of use and application, the ability to provide you with more control over your life, reductions in problem solving time, and reductions in the stress and uncertainty that often accompany problem solving situations. Although research has not been conducted to support all of these advantages, there is evidence that CPS can be more effective than some other problem solving approaches.

The future of CPS should involve greater application of the model, increased use of computer applications, additional refinements to the model, research on the effectiveness of various techniques that supplement stages of the model, and research on the effectiveness of the model in different situations and when different evaluation criteria are used.

Trainers who introduce the model might begin by dealing with expectations of the class and discussing differences in learning styles and their impact upon problem solving. A "guided tour" of the model, led by a facilitator, also could be useful if the class is led through each stage and not too much detail is involved.

A brief discussion on problem types might help the class better understand appropriate uses of the model. Use a variety of examples when conducting this discussion. However, you might spend less time on other introductory topics, since they are not as important during an initial presentation. To increase motivation, get your audience involved.

2

Creative Thinking Climates

Al Lynn (not his real name) is an export sales representative for a large chemical corporation. Although he is not a chemist and has only one year of college, his job requires him to have considerable knowledge about a variety of chemical products. Because of his knowledge and his interactions with a variety of customers, Al often thinks of potential new chemical products.

Recently, Al thought of a new product that could be developed by combining two chemical compounds produced by his company. If successful, the resulting product would have a high potential for success in the international market.

Al presented his idea to a technician in the company. The technician said that the compounds could not be combined because they would explode. Al decided to persevere and seek a second opinion. He went to another technician who also happened to be a friend. His friend told him that the first technician was right.

Al refused to be dismayed. His intuition and limited knowledge of chemistry told him that the compounds could be mixed together without any major problems. So, he asked the technicians to test the chemicals for him. Somewhat reluctantly, they agreed.

After taking numerous safety precautions, the technicians mixed together the compounds. Nothing happened. Not even a whimper. Although somewhat surprised by the outcome, the technicians advised Al that water could not be added to the mixture. It definitely would explode. To demonstrate, they told Al to stand back while they added water to the mixture. As the water was added, the chemical mixture became wet. And that was all. No explosion. No fire. Nothing.

The sales representative with one year of college was right. However, his problems were not over. He still had to persuade the company that there was a market for his product. With little support, Al eventually succeeded. But his success came only after several international markets expressed a strong interest in his product. Then, his company became interested.

If all people, groups, organizations, and societies made optimal use of their creative potential, there probably wouldn't be much need for books such as this one. If we all were just as creative as we could be, we could solve most of our problems with little difficulty. And we wouldn't need to learn new processes and techniques.

Unfortunately, individuals, groups, organizations, and societies are not optimally creative. We always have struggled and will continue to struggle to develop creative solutions for our most difficult problems. Our world is imperfect and probably always will be.

We don't struggle because we lack information on how to solve problems. Dealing with everyday types of problems has given us experience in how to resolve them. For example, you probably don't panic when faced with the problem of keeping dry while walking in the rain. Experience has taught you that an umbrella and raincoat will help.

Struggling enters the picture only when we face problems for which we have no custom-made solutions. For these problems we are forced to overcome barriers that block our ability to develop different problem perspectives. Thus, if you are a training director faced with the problem of convincing higher management of the importance of your department, you might struggle a bit to come up with an adequate response.

We often struggle because the creative climates we live in are inappropriate environments for dealing with hard-to-solve problems. Optimal use of our creative potential requires climates conducive to creative thinking. Al Lynn's situation is a perfect example of this need.

The climates we need to be creative are both external and internal to us. Although related, it is important to consider these climates separately. This way, it will be easier to understand the major factors involved.

External climates refer to perceptions we have about things in our external environment that affect our ability to perform creatively. In organizations, our external climates consist of such things as procedures, policies, rewards and punishments, communication channels, supplies, equipment, and co-worker attitudes.

Internal climates are the psychological and mental attributes we possess that help determine our ability to function creatively. We have a positive internal creative climate if we are motivated to become more creative, are open to new experiences, and so forth. A negative internal climate, in contrast, would be characterized by a closed mind that is not prepared to deal with newness.

In general, it is more important to have a positive internal climate than a positive external climate. If you possess the internal resources needed to become more creative and deal with your problems creatively, you should be able to cope with a relatively negative external climate. However, if your internal climate is generally negative and your external climate positive, you may experience trouble solving problems creatively. Although the external conditions exist, creativity starts from within the individual.

All is not lost, however. With minimal internal motivation, use of the CPS process and appropriate techniques, many deficiencies of a negative internal climate can be overcome. The key element in such situations is motivation. If you don't have the necessary internal motivation needed to be creative and solve your problems, it won't matter how conducive your external environment is.

Awareness of and understanding about internal and external climates is essential for using the CPS process effectively. Knowing about the specific factors involved in these climates sometimes can help in overcoming many creative thinking obstacles. The remainder of this chapter is concerned with some major internal and external factors. Although not exhaustive, these factors should give you at least a rough notion of what is involved.

EXTERNAL FACTORS

The environment in your organization is likely to be conducive to creative thinking if it can be characterized as described in the following section (VanGundy, 1984). The first listing contains external factors involving task-related elements in the environment; the second listing is concerned with people-related environmental elements.

1. *Provide freedom to do things differently.* Although a lot of organizations provide certain employees freedom to try new approaches, a lot only give lip service to this factor. If employees feel free to experiment, the results sometimes can be surprising. A large cosmetics company, for example, allowed some of its employees the freedom to play around with their own ideas for new products. An innovative way to apply makeup was developed and is now being marketed successfully.

Such freedom does not mean that total anarchy should be permitted. Some organizational tasks require routine thinking and should be permitted to function that way. When appropriate, however, the general feeling should be that new ideas are welcome. Moreover, organizations should provide the internal mechanisms required to give these ideas a fair hearing. The Kodak Company is an excellent example of an organization that has developed specific procedures for handling new ideas (Rosenfeld, 1982). At Kodak, an office of innovation has been set up to process employee ideas for new ways of doing things.

2. *Maintain an optimal amount of work pressure.* To make the best use of our creative potential, our external environments should contain an optimal

amount of work pressure. Too much pressure to perform can increase stress and block creative ideas; too little pressure can decrease motivation to be creative. In any case, the organization should strive to maintain just enough pressure to get the job done and allow freedom for creative thinking. The slave driver manager is no longer appropriate. We now need "creative" driving managers—creative people who can manage other creative people.

3. *Provide realistic work goals.* Depending upon which theory of motivation you like, goals may play an important role in how you view human performance. According to some psychologists, we can attain maximum performance if we are motivated by specific goals that we perceive to be both challenging and realistic (e.g., Latham & Kinne, 1974). If goals are perceived as unrealistic, however, goal setting may backfire. Trying to achieve something seen as too difficult can result in frustration and downturns in performance and job satisfaction. Creative performance requires the right amount of goal achievement for each individual.

4. *Use a low level of supervision.* Many supervisors—perhaps because they are new in the job or because of some quirk in their personality—often tend to "oversupervise." They perceive the burden for task accomplishment to lie solely on their shoulders. When some employees receive more directions and orders than they expect, rebellion often occurs. This rebellion may take place as covert resentment and general dissatisfaction or it may be more open in the form of strikes or sabotage. Whatever the form, supervisors should try to minimize control in areas requiring creative thinking.

5. *Delegate responsibilities.* In general, people can be more creative when they perceive themselves to have some degree of control over their jobs. It is very difficult to be creative when you constantly are burdened with minute details. If you spend all of your time "stamping out small fires," you never will develop an effective strategy for managing fires. You must have some freedom to do planning, even if it is a small amount of time. The best way to allow yourself this freedom is to delegate as much responsibility as you can.

If you are a manager, delegating responsibility requires trust in your subordinates. I don't believe that anyone should automatically trust all subordinates to be capable of performing all tasks equally well. That is a somewhat naive view of human nature. Although all "normal" people may have the potential to perform well, the fact is that they all don't. Whether for lack of motivation or basic skills, all people are just not alike in their abilities. As a result, you need to know how much responsibility your subordinates can handle. Don't ration responsibility too much, however. The job does need to get done.

6. *Encourage participation.* Some research has shown that performance and satisfaction can be enhanced when employees participate in setting goals (e.g., Latham & Yukl, 1976). This participation, however, probably is not as important as the actual setting of the goals. Nevertheless, there does seem

to be a positive relationship between participation in decision making and satisfaction with the final solution (e.g., Carey, 1972; Coch & French, 1948). It also is likely that allowing people to participate in decision making may increase, in some cases, the self-confidence needed for creative thought and behavior.

7. *Provide immediate and timely feedback.* Although goal setting is an important element in task performance, there is some evidence that feedback will further enhance any benefits derived from goal setting alone (Kim & Hammer, 1976). Employees not only should be allowed to assist in setting goals, they also should have the opportunity to see the results of their efforts. To be useful, feedback must be received about the same time that behavior occurs. In addition, the feedback must come at a time when it can be of most use.

Feedback can be very important during the CPS process. CPS often involves frequent adjustments in activities throughout the six stages. For instance, information for defining a problem might not become available until after you have left the problem-finding stage. If the information should appear during solution-finding or acceptance-finding, you may want to return to problem-finding. However, in some cases, it may be too late to make needed adjustments and you will have to respond as well as you can.

Timing of feedback cannot always be controlled. If possible, feedback should be provided as soon as it becomes available and it is practical to disseminate it. Unfortunately, the bureaucratic structure of many organizations often makes it difficult for this to happen.

8. *Provide necessary resources and support.* This final external task factor is almost a "given." It should go without saying that creativity requires a minimal level of resources and support. You must have the money, time, people, information, supplies, and other items needed to accomplish your job. Without these, you cannot expect to maximize your creative potential. In fact, when resources are in short supply, you may exhaust your creative energies in trying to offset the imbalance. As a result, you might have little energy left for more productive tasks.

The list of external factors that follows is concerned primarily with people-related elements that should be present in an organization. In general, the climate of the organization will be characterized as positive in this area if it:

1. *Encourages open expression of ideas.* A general feeling that the organization is open and receptive to ideas must be perceived by people before they will feel free to suggest ideas. Like most aspects of creative climates in organizations, more than lip service must be given to openness. Upper management must state and then demonstrate its commitment to the production of creative ideas.

2. *Accepts "off the wall" ideas.* To be perceived as having a positive climate, an organization may need to tolerate what often are viewed as unconven-

tional ideas. Individual differences among people usually assure that not everyone in an organization will propose similar types of ideas. These differences must be respected. Moreover, these differences should be viewed as a valuable resource. Because people have different ways of looking at situations, different problem perspectives can be provided. In most cases, having a variety of perspectives will increase the odds of developing workable solutions to problems.

3. *Provides assistance in developing ideas.* Most brilliant ideas were not originally thought of in their final form. Instead, they required a considerable amount of polishing before they were considered to be fully developed.

In organizations, employees' ideas should not be treated as if they must be in a final form. Often, a few modifications can transform an initially "bad" idea into one more workable. This is not to say, however, that employee ideas always should be accepted. Employees should be encouraged to submit the best ideas possible. But it also must be understood that many ideas will have to be rejected. Between submission and rejection, ideas should be given a fair hearing and allowed to develop as much as feasible.

4. *Encourages risk taking.* This factor probably is one of the most important elements in a creative climate. Employees should feel free to take risks when proposing ideas and not fear that their careers will be jeopardized for doing so. This does not mean that anything goes. Rather, the atmosphere should be one that permits calculated risk taking. Management also has a major responsibility in encouraging risk taking. Because of the potential costs to the employee, management somehow must buffer any potential negative consequences of risk taking. This might be as simple as setting an example of openness to new ideas or as complex as designing a formal system to ensure that all ideas receive a fair hearing.

5. *Provides time for individual efforts.* CPS requires time to think and consider many different possibilities. If employees aren't provided with some time for personal thinking or can't create it on their own, there will be limited opportunities for them to exercise their creativity. Furthermore, some employees are more motivated when they have the chance to pursue projects in which they have a personal interest. As long as it is in the best interest of the company, these employees need to feel that they will be rewarded for pursuing individual projects and given the time to do so.

6. *Encourages professional growth and development.* Because of the temporary character of most forms of knowledge, most professionals must constantly strive to keep up to date in their fields. Unfortunately, the press of day-to-day work often makes this an impossible task. As a result, organizations should encourage employees to grow within their jobs. Ways to do this might include: attending conferences and workshops, refresher courses at universities, or executive sabbaticals in which leaves are granted for new learning and personal renewal.

7. *Encourages interaction with others outside the work group.* Groups who

work together over time and are allowed to function without much outside influence often develop "groupthink" (Janis, 1972). This is a condition in which groups exhibit a high degree of perceived cohesion and suspend critical thinking. They may begin to see themselves as incapable of any wrongdoing. All of their decisions are "right" because they developed them.

Although some research suggests that groupthink may occur only with members low in dominant behavior (Callaway, Marriott & Esser, 1985), too much confidence in any group has the potential to make problem solving difficult. This is especially true for groups using CPS.

Because creativity requires new viewpoints, all groups should seek out other viewpoints. Outsiders can offer new perspectives that can reduce some of the negative outcomes associated with cohesion.

8. *Recognizes the value of ideas.* Although internal motivation is critical for creative thinking, some degree of external reinforcement also can be helpful. If you believe that your ideas are worthy of consideration, you probably will be more satisfied in your job (or at least you can maintain your current level of satisfaction). Moreover, sensing that your organization values your ideas can motivate you to suggest additional ideas.

9. *Exhibits confidence in the workers.* This factor is important because of its ability to produce a positive, self-fulfilling prophecy. If you constantly are told by your organization that you are creative, then you are more likely to believe it and produce creative products. This is a relatively low cost way for any organization to encourage creative thinking. Unfortunately, it often is overlooked due to the politics and bureaucratic aspects of organizational life.

INTERNAL FACTORS

As important as external factors may be, they are only of secondary importance when compared to internal factors. As I noted previously in this chapter, creativity starts from within the individual. Many of the dysfunctional aspects of our external environments can be overcome with an open mind and a positive attitude.

In no particular order, major factors involved in positive, internal creative climates are:

1. *Openness to new ideas.* To be fully creative, our minds must be receptive to new ideas. Even if we disagree with them or find little value in them, all ideas can serve as stimulators for new ideas. In working with CPS groups, one of my most difficult tasks as a facilitator is to encourage individuals to consider the positive aspects of all ideas before evaluating them. To be closed to new ideas is to live in the past, while trying to solve problems in the present for the future.

2. *Curiosity.* Like young children, creative people constantly ask questions about their environments. Solving problems creatively requires that many different questions be asked. Supposedly, one reason Albert Einstein

achieved so many insights was his ability to ask a lot of different questions. In particular, Einstein seemed to be a master at questioning the obvious. By questioning what others often accepted at face value (or paid no attention to) he could extend the range of his problem solving ability. We all can do the same by trying to become more curious.

3. *Independence.* To develop new problem perspectives, it helps if you are an independent thinker. If you are overly influenced by the opinions of others, you will be more likely to view problems in conventional ways. When working with CPS groups, it usually is easy to spot independent thinkers. They are not afraid to express their own viewpoints and frequently will become involved in heated discussions. (However, don't equate verbal aggressiveness with independent thinking.)

4. *Perseverence.* Al Lynn, discussed at the beginning of this chapter, is an excellent example of someone who perseveres. He persisted in exploring his new product idea in spite of the resistance he met from the experts. In the public mind, the one person who probably best typifies the persevering creative spirit is Thomas Edison. He often is quoted as having said that "genius is 98 percent perspiration and 2 percent inspiration." A lot of hard work is involved in thinking of and developing creative ideas.

5. *Risk taking.* Many people would argue that you never will produce anything creative unless you take risks. This is especially true in the business world. Although imitation may be the "sincerest form of flattery," it is not always a productive way to generate new business ideas. The producer of the "Pet Rock," for example, took considerable risks to market his product and was quite successful. However, a series of imitators soon followed, none of which achieved even close to the same degree of financial success.

Risk taking does not mean that anything goes and that you should throw caution to the wind. Rather, risk taking should be a calculated endeavor. The military has a saying that probably best captures what I am trying to say: "There are old pilots and there are bold pilots, but there are no old, bold pilots."

6. *Discipline.* It almost appears paradoxical to say that creative thinking requires discipline. For many people, creative problem solving involves wild and reckless thinking and "off the wall" ideas. In many respects, CPS does require this type of thinking and ideas. However, there also is a more structured side to the process.

To produce unique ideas, you must attack your problems with the discipline needed to diverge and converge within each stage of the model. A freewheeling type of thinking is involved, but it certainly should not dominate the entire process.

7. *Playfulness.* Most new ideas just don't spring forth in full bloom. Instead, we usually need to play around with problems and ideas. We need to examine them from many different perspectives. Creative insights can be gained by toying with ideas and looking at them in detail. Playfulness

also is important in groups and individuals as an overall attitude toward a problem solving task. If you ever observe or participate in a group that seems to produce a large number of ideas, one feature that distinguishes it from other groups is its playful attitude.

8. *Impulsiveness.* Contrary to what we sometimes are taught, jumping to conclusions can be beneficial when solving problems. Instead of withholding your opinions and feelings about problem situations, you sometimes must be free to exercise judgment. During the CPS process, this feeling is particularly important during convergent activities. You also need to feel free to be impulsive during divergent activities. When diverging, you should generate all the data you can without initially judging it. Say or think whatever pops into your mind and write it down. Save your judgment for later.

SUGGESTIONS FOR TRAINERS

It is difficult to change the various climates within people, groups, and organizations. This is especially true when a climate involves factors conducive to creative thinking and problem solving. These factors are so deeply ingrained that most people are highly resistant to change.

For most of us, changing the way we perceive and react to situations would require a major readjustment in our personalities—a feat that would be extremely difficult if not impossible. Obviously, just having someone like a trainer tell us we should change will not be sufficient. Instead, we need to be self-motivated—motivated from within ourselves.

In spite of the formidable obstacles presented by trying to change creative climates, a discussion of the nature and nurture of creative climates might at least help increase awareness about their importance. In many respects, a positive climate may be more important than learning a problem solving process and associated techniques. If you don't approach a problem with the appropriate attitudes and perceptions, you won't receive the full benefit from problem solving models and techniques. Using creativity methods without the proper approach would be like buying tools to build a house without any knowledge of construction methods and techniques.

Improving upon creative climates is obviously not an easy task. Simply reading about some of the major factors involved will not be enough. Change will be more likely if you have a chance to analyze creative climate factors relevant to your situation and then devise a specific action plan for improving them.

Conducting a discussion on creative climates. One way to introduce the topic of creative climates is to divide your class into groups of five or six people. Ask the groups to spend 10 or 15 minutes discussing the general nature of a creative climate and their definition of it. When the time is up, have the groups reconvene and present their definitions and interpretations. If possible, write them down on flipchart paper or a chalkboard. Note any major similarities and dissimilarities between the results of the groups. Then, ask the class to help you categorize the results in terms of internal and external factors.

As a follow-up to this exercise, you also might have the group note instances in which the internal factors might affect (or be related to) the external factors and vice versa. For instance, an internal factor such as independence should be related closely to an external factor such as delegation of responsibilities or provision of time for individual efforts.

To help the class members relate better to the concept of creative climates, you also might have them break into small groups and examine their own work situations. For example, you might ask them to break into groups again and discuss how conducive to creativity: they are internally, their work unit is, and their organization is. Ask them to be as specific as possible when doing this exercise. Encourage them to list many different examples. Then, have them develop lists of the factors that encourage or discourage creative climates within themselves, their work units, or their organization. Then, have them reconvene to share and discuss their results.

Developing action plans. The exercises previously described are designed to increase understanding of the nature and importance of creative climates. However, they also will help to increase awareness of the climates currently prevailing within the participants and their organization. If this increased awareness results in a perception that the climates are less positive than desired, you might suggest that the class consider acting upon some possible changes.

After being divided into groups, the class might deal with these changes (especially for groups and the organization) using the following instructions:

1. Describe what climate currently exists in your regular work group or the total organization. Be specific and list as many factors as you can. Narrow down the number of items by assigning priorities.
2. Describe the climate you would like to have (i.e., the ideal climate). As with the first list, identify priorities.
3. Develop specific action plans for making the current climate more like the ideal climate. If possible, consider implementation obstacles and how they might be overcome. When generating plans, delay all judgment.
4. Sort the plans into those that can be implemented in the short term (e.g., within six months to a year) and those that will require long-term action.
5. Generate a list of criteria for judging the action plans. These criteria might include such things as time required, financial costs, number of people required, and control over the problem area. Delay all judgment when generating these criteria.
6. Evaluate the short- and long-term plans and select the best plans within each

category. As part of these plans, include a provision for follow-up activities. If required, assign one or more people to monitor these activities.

Once the groups have finished this exercise, have them reconvene and share their lists. If time permits, they might try to agree upon priority areas and the best ways to improve various climate factors. However, don't expect unanimous consent. The most optimistic outcome might be identification of areas of convergence and agreement upon major actions required.

SUMMARY

The world in general is not optimally conducive to creative thinking and problem solving. As individuals, groups, and organizations, we usually struggle to deal with difficult problems that require creative solutions—solutions that must be custom-made. A major reason we struggle with these problems is because our personal and work climates often are not appropriate for solving problems creatively.

Creativity climates are both internal and external to us. External climates are those aspects of our environments that affect our ability to solve problems creatively. Internal climates are composed of the psychological attitudes we all possess that influence our creative problem solving abilities. In general, it is better to have a positive internal climate and negative external climate than the other way around. A motivated individual with the proper attitudes toward creative thinking frequently can overcome many environmental obstacles to creative problem solving. Finally, internal and external climates are interrelated and there is considerable overlap between them.

Task-related elements for a positive external climate include such things as: freedom to do things differently, an optimal amount of work pressure, realistic work goals, a low level of supervision, delegation of responsibilities, encouragement to participate in decision making, timely and immediate feedback on job performance, and provision of all required resources and support systems.

People-related factors needed for a positive external environment include such things as: an atmosphere that encourages open expression of ideas, acceptance of "off-the-wall" ideas, assistance in developing ideas, encouragement to take realistic risks, provision for time to pursue individual projects, opportunities for professional growth and development, interaction with others outside the work group, recognition of the value of new ideas, and demonstration of confidence in workers.

Some major internal factors needed for a creative climate are: openness to new ideas, curiosity, independence, perseverance, risk taking, discipline, ability to play with ideas, and impulsiveness.

3
Creative Thinking Exercises: Part I

As I noted in Chapter 2, our internal and external creative climates are important determinants of our ability to solve problems creatively. Simply reading about the ingredients involved in these climates, however, may not be enough to understand their importance fully.

This chapter and Chapter 4 present 25 exercises to demonstrate some major creative thinking principles and abilities. The first three sets of exercises are designed to illustrate the importance of testing assumptions, looking for the positive in ideas, and self- and problem-awareness (Exercises 1 through 12). The remaining exercises, presented in Chapter 4, deal with basic abilities involved in creative thinking: fluency, flexibility, and originality (Exercises 13 through 25). Answers and comments about the exercises are presented at the end of each chapter.

The categories used to present these exercises are somewhat arbitrary. Other categories could have been used. Moreover, there is quite a bit of overlap among the categories. For example, both ideational fluency and flexibility are closely related. Therefore, you probably should not regard the categories as being fixed and rigid.

Creative thinking exercises are important to creativity in much the same way that warm-up exercises are important to physical exercises. Just as the body needs to be warmed up before intense physical exertion, so does the mind need to be limbered up before creative problem solving. Much of our day-to-day problem solving involves analytical skills that can't always be turned off quickly. Instead, we often need to work our way gradually into a creative mode of thinking.

Developing a creative thinking mode, however, involves more than just reading some exercises. You must become actively involved and expect to increase your creative thinking powers. If you wanted to increase your physical performance in some area, you wouldn't expect to see much improvement if you bought an exercise video tape and faithfully watched it every day from your easy chair. You have to become involved! The same holds true for creative thinking. You must take an active role in your own development and expect to improve yourself.

EXERCISES FOR TESTING ASSUMPTIONS

The ability to fully test assumptions about a problem situation may be one of the most important of all problem solving skills. Maier (1963) has noted that effective problem solving is more likely to occur when we are problem-minded rather than solution-minded. That is, we need to make an effort to be sure we understand a problem before proposing solutions to resolve it. After all, finding a solution is easy once you fully understand the problem. As I have noted elsewhere, an understood problem is a solved problem (VanGundy, 1986).

The only way we can fully understand our problems is to test all the assumptions we make about them. Contrary to much popular thinking, testing assumptions is far more important than generating ideas. It is easy to generate ideas, but it is an entirely different matter to know if you are generating ideas for the "right" problem. As Einstein noted:

The formulation of a problem is often more essential than its solution which may be merely a matter of mathematical or experimental skill. To raise new questions, new possibilities, to regard old questions from a new angle, requires creative imagination and marks real advance in science [Einstein and Infeld, 1938, p. 29].

Somewhat more to the point, Wertheimer (1959, p. 123) has observed that: "Often in great discoveries the most important thing is that a certain question is found. Envisaging, putting the productive question is often more important, often a greater achievement than solution of a set question."

An excellent illustration of the importance of testing problem assumptions is provided in a story developed by Dillon, Schwartz, and Smilansky and reported by Getzels (1975).

A car was travelling down a deserted road in the countryside when it blew a tire. After opening the car's trunk, the driver and his passengers discover that the jack is missing. They decided to define their problem as: "How might we obtain a jack?" They remembered a service station in a town they had just driven through and decided to walk to it to borrow a jack. Then, they would walk back to the car, change the tire, drive back to town and return the jack, and then turn around and resume their trip.

Just as they began walking toward town, another car came along from the opposite direction. Amazingly, it too blew a tire in almost the same location as the first car. Even more amazingly (and quite conveniently for the purposes of this story), the occupants of the second car discovered that the jack to their car also was missing. However, instead of defining their problem in terms of how to obtain a jack, the occupants of this car decided to define their problem as: "How might we raise our car?" Looking around, they spotted a nearby barn with a pulley used for lifting bales of hay. They pushed the car to the barn, raised it with the pulley, changed the tire, and resumed their trip. Shortly after they started driving again, they passed the occupants of the first car, still walking toward town.

Getzels notes that it is tempting to comment that the occupants of the second car developed a clever solution. However, a better observation is that they developed an even more clever question. The unique solution of using a pulley to raise their car was a direct result of the assumptions they made in defining their problem (i.e., they assumed that their primary problem was to raise the car). In marked contrast, the occupants of the first car restricted their solution alternatives by assuming that their primary problem was to obtain a jack.

In one respect, this illustration has implications for people involved in educating and training others. We can help people acquire knowledge, but it is difficult to teach them how to use this knowledge to solve problems. Moreover, it is even more difficult to help people discover problems. Unfortunately, as Thelen (1972) has observed, educational systems often view their mission as starting where someone else has defined the problem. To be fully functioning individuals, we need the ability to discover our own problems. Teaching someone tricks for generating ideas rarely is sufficient.

There are a number of relatively simple exercises that can demonstrate the importance of testing problem assumptions. Most of these exercises have been around for years. It is possible that you already may be familiar with some or all of them. Even so, you should take the time to examine the major principles they illustrate.

Answers (when appropriate) and comments for all the exercises are in the section of this chapter titled, "Exercise Answers and Comments."

Exercise 1. What is half of eight? Write down as many answers as you can think of.

Exercise 2. Without looking at it, draw a picture of your watch. If you don't have a watch, draw a picture of any clock with hands that you look at every day.

Exercise 3. Draw a circle and pretend it is a top view of a pie. Then, draw lines to show how you might cut this pie into eight pieces using only three cuts. If you are successful using three cuts, try using only two cuts.

Exercise 4. How many squares are shown in Figure 3–1? Are you sure you have the correct answer?

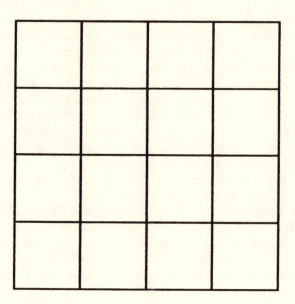

Figure 3–1
The Square Problem

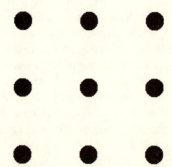

Figure 3–2
The Nine-Dot Problem

Exercise 5. Using nine dots arranged as those shown in figure 3–2, connect all of the dots using no more than four straight lines. You may not lift up your pen or pencil or retrace any lines.

POSITIVE ATTITUDE EXERCISES

In Chapter 2 I discussed how important positive internal and external creative climates are to creative problem solving. The two exercises in this

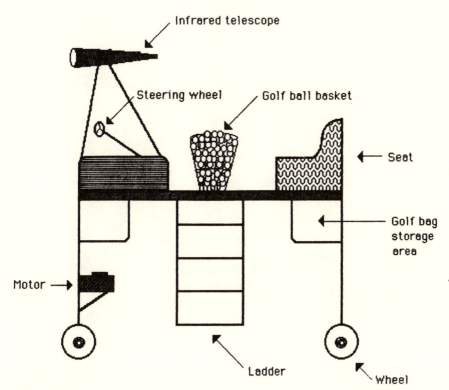

Figure 3–3
Golf Cart Design

section stress the importance of positive thinking during both the divergent and convergent phases of CPS.

Exercise 6. Write down as many improvements as you can think of for a common household flashlight. Allow yourself five minutes to do this.

Exercise 7. Write down as many comments as you can about my design for a golf cart shown in Figure 3–3.

The next set of exercises is concerned with some basic creative thinking abilities: awareness, fluency, flexibility, and originality.

AWARENESS EXERCISES

To be an effective problem solver, you need to be aware of yourself, your environment, and your problems. Just knowing that a problem exists is not enough. You must understand all the relevant bits of information that can affect your ability to solve problems creatively. You must be able to separate the important from the unimportant and identify those problem features that can help you develop a unique perspective. To do this, you

1000
40
1000
30
1000
20
1000
10
———

Figure 3–4
Addition Exercise

need to have general awareness of yourself and your environment and specific awareness of a particular problem.

The following exercises will help you evaluate your general awareness and help you practice awareness of specific problems. After you complete each exercise, try to think of at least one positive thing you learned from the exercise.

Exercise 8. A series of numbers is presented in figure 3–4. Try to avoid looking at the numbers right now. Using a piece of paper or cardboard, cover them all up except the first one. Your task is to add up the numbers as they appear. Read aloud as you add. For instance, if the first three numbers are 50, 25, and 10, you would say, "50, 75, 85," and so forth until you have added up all the numbers. Remember, reveal only one number at a time.

Exercise 9. What do the following numbers have in common: 1, 4, 9, 16, 25, 36, 49, 64?

Exercise 10. Without actually being in it, describe your favorite room where you live. Describe it in as much detail as possible. Try to go beyond mere physical descriptions of objects in the room.

Exercise 11. Select an object and pretend you are it. Describe how you are used, how you might affect other people or things, how you might change or stay the same, how you could be used in a different way, and so forth. Try to use as many senses as possible in doing this exercise.

Exercise 12. I borrowed this exercise from Stevens (1971). He refers to it as "reversal identification." It is similar to some of the activities used in the previous exercise, but is a little more abstract. If possible, you should have someone else direct you in this exercise.

Begin by lying down in a comfortable position. Close your eyes and try to relax as much as possible. Allow any built-up tension to leave your body.

Next, concentrate upon your breathing. Notice everything you can about how you breathe—how it moves in and out your nose or mouth; how it moves down your throat and then causes your chest or stomach to rise and fall. Become aware as possible of your breathing.

Now, try to reverse the whole process. Imagine that you no longer are breathing air. Instead, try to experience the air breathing you. As you do this, feel the air move into your lungs and then leave. Relax. You do not have to participate in your breathing now. Then, instead of the air breathing you, switch back to you breathing the air. Experience the difference.

As another exercise in reversal identification, select some activity in your life—something with which you are very familiar. For example, you might select something like shopping or a meeting you attend regularly. Try to visualize and experience the actual sequence of events involved in performing this activity. Once you have spent some time doing this, reverse the activity. Visualize and experience the sequence of events in reverse. Then, evaluate your experience. Did you change any perceptions you had of yourself? Is there anything about yourself that you like or dislike more? Do you think that this reversal method might help you solve some problems? Why or why not?

EXERCISE ANSWERS AND COMMENTS

Exercise 1: The "creative" response to this exercise is based upon the assumption that there is more than one "correct" answer possible. Moreover, you should not assume that the solution has to be mathematical. Mathematics is only one way to solve certain types of problems. Other problem solving strategies can be of equal or greater value, depending upon the nature of the problem. If you had trouble thinking of more than one answer, you might have been trying to solve a problem involving the "number" eight, rather than the symbol used to represent it.

In addition to the number four, other possible answers to the exercise include: "VI"(half of the Roman numeral VIII), "II" (the other half of the same Roman numeral), "zero" (the top or bottom half of the number 8), "eig" ("half" of the word "eight") "ht" (the other "half" of the word "eight"), and "eight" (the result of drawing a horizontal line through the word). Of course, there are many other possibilities.

Exercise 2: Successful completion of this exercise requires a good memory and excellent visualization skills. Your watch is something you look at every day. However, you probably are so familiar with it that you fail to notice most of the details involved. For example, my watch has the word "quartz" right above the number "6." This word is not the type of information I want when I look at my watch. As a result, I rarely take the time to notice anything on my watch unrelated to the time.

We frequently assume we are familiar with something and then are surprised to find out how unfamiliar we are when put to the test. This is especially true during creative problem solving. Perhaps because of a need to make order out of chaos, we often assume we know more about a

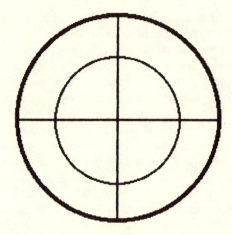

Figure 3–5
Solution to the Pie Problem

problem situation than we actually do. Testing such assumptions carefully is the only way to overcome this habit.

Exercise 3: What did you assume about this exercise? If you came up with at least one solution using two or three cuts, you were forced to test some basic assumptions we all seem to take for granted about pies. If you could not solve this problem, you failed to test these assumptions. Look again at the instructions. Test the assumptions you are making about each word. What limitations are you placing upon yourself that are not part of the problem? For example, what is meant by the words "cut" and "pieces"?

What originally was billed as the "correct" solution is shown in Figure 3–5. The "trick," of course, is that nothing was said to require you to use straight lines or limit yourself to wedge-shaped pieces. These both were limitations that you placed upon yourself—not limitations imposed by the problem as it was presented. Two alternate solutions are shown in figure 3–6. Figure 3–6a shows a solution for which many other variations also are possible. Figure 3–6b shows a solution using only two cuts, from which other variations also could be developed.

Exercise 4: The basic approach needed to solve this exercise is similar to that needed for the pie problem. Ask yourself what assumptions you are making. If you try to deal with this problem mathematically, you may be blocked. Such problems might be familiar, since they often are used in elementary school math texts to illustrate basic multiplication concepts. For example, in a four-by-four two-dimensional matrix, you can multiply the number of squares on each side to find the total product. To arrive at a solution other than 16, you need to make the problem unfamiliar. That is, you need to ask yourself how a "square" might be defined in this case.

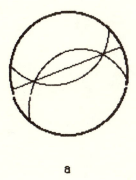

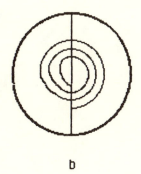

a   b

Figure 3–6
Other Pie Problem Solutions

Need more help? No one said that the lines could not be used more than once.

The solution obviously requires you to redefine your perceptions of a square. If you view the picture as containing 16 squares, then that is all you will see. However, if you assume that you can use each line more than once, a number of solution possibilities are opened up.

For instance, the border of the drawing is a square, there are nine two-by-two squares, four three-by-three squares, one large square formed by the 10 border squares, and four three-by-three squares that use the small squares as borders. Including the 16 "original" squares, there could be a total of 35 squares. However, the drawing appears to contain only two dimensions. If a third dimension is considered, the number of squares possible is infinite. What you see in the figure may be only a slice of a square shape that extends to infinity (or curves back around, depending upon your view of the universe).

Exercise 5: This exercise can be a tough one. Not too many people are able to solve it without prior experience or adequate hints. For example, in one study involving 128 introductory pyschology students, less than 10 percent were able to solve it without some help (Lung & Dominowski, 1985). Don't let this deter you. After all, you probably aren't an introductory psychology student.

A typical hint involves drawing lines outside of the "square" formed by the shape of the dots. That is, don't confine your lines within this square, but try extending them beyond its boundaries. If this hint doesn't help, try starting from a point outside the square. Another hint is to feel free to connect lines at intersecting points outside of the square. That is, every time you stop drawing one line and begin another, you don't "have" to do it on one of the dots.

Give up? What is usually considered to be the "correct" solution is shown

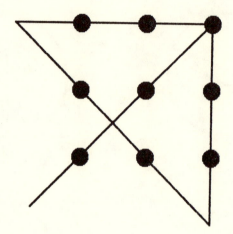

Figure 3–7
Solution to the Nine-Dot Problem

in Figure 3–7. If you haven't seen this solution before, you may have experienced an "aha!" when you first saw it. Adams (1979, pp. 24–32) illustrates some other possible solutions to this problem. For example, he notes that the problem can be solved with three straight lines (Figure 3–8a), or even with one straight line (Figure 3–8b). The solution in Figure 3–8a is achieved by observing that the lines do not have to go through the centers of the dots; the solution in Figure 3–8b is based upon the notion that the dots can be cut up and rearranged. Another one-line solution is to increase the width of your line so that it covers all nine dots in one pass.

Exercises 6 and 7: Both the positive and the negative are important during the CPS process. However, we sometimes use positive and negative thinking inappropriately. Most of us cannot be accused of spending too much time praising ideas when we should be evaluating them (such as during convergent activities). Instead, we are more likely to be guilty of being critical when we should be more positive (such as during divergent activities).

There are several positive comments or new ideas that might be suggested by the negative features in the golf cart design. The misplaced steering wheel suggests an emergency brake or a valve for ballast when crossing a lake. The raised platform suggests advantages for seeing the flag from a distance, going through water and mud, avoiding animals on the course (e.g., alligators in Florida), playing over other players (as opposed to playing "through" them), and determining if other players are about finished putting. The ladder suggests a hydraulic lift for raising and lowering the platform. The telescope, although apparently practical, also suggests using a video camera to help improve your swing and to pinpoint the exact location where a ball went out of bounds. Finally, the small wheels suggest clustering

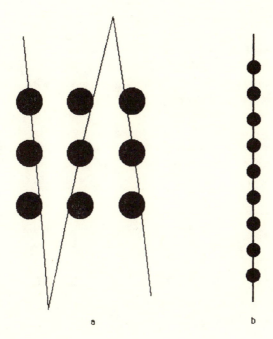

a   b

Figure 3–8
Alternate Nine-Dot Problem Solutions

a number of such wheels to make an all-terrain vehicle. Similar types of comments could also be made about the positive and negative features of an improved flashlight.

Exercise 8: This exercise is deceptively simple. Many people initially assume that it is too easy for them and below their ability (as a result, they usually are somewhat suspicious). And then they see the correct answer. When they see that they added the numbers incorrectly, their awareness level suddenly collapses. Disbelief is a common reaction. In contrast to some of the previous exercises, there is supposed to be one correct answer to this problem and they missed it!

In case you haven't figured it out by now, the correct answer is 4,100. If you are like many others, you probably said 5,000 when you first added them.

You probably are a little upset with yourself if you answered this problem incorrectly. You may be asking yourself what went wrong. The answer lies in the tendency of the human mind to become trapped into patterned ways of thinking and behaving. We sometimes become locked on a particular course of action before we are aware of it. That is what usually happens with this exercise. We lose our awareness about the patterns we follow.

Exercise 9: You probably were able to come up with one solution to this exercise by noting that the numbers are squares of consecutive numbers between one and seven (e.g., $1^2 = 1$, $2^2 = 4$, $3^2 = 9$). If this was your only answer, you were taken in by a pattern. However, unlike the addition exercise in Exercise 8, more than one answer is readily apparent (this is not to say that some creative person could not come up with multiple answers for Exercise 8). To see these answers you must break away from the pattern based upon squares of numbers. That is, you must be aware that a pattern exists and attempt to break it to explore other potential alternatives.

A relatively simple pattern also is evident by noting that every other number is evenly divisible. A more complicated solution pattern can be constructed using the shapes of the numbers. Some numbers contain straight lines and are open (i.e., no enclosed areas); other numbers are curved and enclosed. Assuming that a two-digit number must possess a minimum of only one number in either category (curved or enclosed), a definite pattern can be observed. The numbers 1 and 4 are both straight line, open numbers; the next two numbers in the series, 9 and 16, both contain curved and enclosed numbers; the third pair contains straight line, open numbers—25 and 36, and so forth.

Exercise 10: What problem solving strategy did you use to deal with this exercise? To develop maximum awareness in this situation, you could use "mixed scanning" (Etzioni, 1968) or, as I call it, "the big picture/little picture" approach. What you do is focus first on the overall scene and try to take in as much information as possible. Next, observe your immediate situation and plot your next step. Then, take action, evaluate the big picture again, and so forth until you have reached your goal or solved the problem.

For instance, picture yourself standing at the edge of an unfamiliar field out in the country. To reach your objective of getting to a point on the other side, you might survey the general territory to pick out the best route. Then, you could start walking and periodically evaluate your progress in reaching your goal.

A similar process can be used to describe your room: try to visualize the entire room in as much detail as possible; focus upon the one wall in the room that is most familiar to you—if it is a large wall, divide it into sections; scrutinize each section of the wall and record everything you see on it and near it (e.g., tables, chairs); visualize the entire room again; and move on to another wall and repeat the process (use the same procedure for the floor and the ceiling).

Exercise 11: This exercise can be difficult for some people. Assuming the identity of an inanimate object is not something most of us do every day. However, the experience of trying can demonstrate the usefulness of adopting another perspective to increase awareness.

People skilled in conflict resolution often use a similar approach. A marriage counselor might ask a married couple, for example, to roleplay the viewpoints of the other spouse. The insights gained from this activity then might be used to form the basis for a plan to reduce or redirect unproductive behavior.

Exercise 12: We sometimes lack awareness of ourselves because of the familiar way we do things. We quite naturally don't notice everything unique to ourselves. As a result, we often are surprised when someone points out one of our peculiarities.

Our problems affect us and are affected by us in much the same way. Because we often are so close to them, it can be difficult to understand them completely. Consciously attempting to reverse our perceptions sometimes can enable us to develop different perspectives we can use to develop creative solutions. Thus, we can help ourselves point out peculiarities in our problems.

Stevens (1971) notes that we all have images of ourselves that are only partially true. Using a technique such as reversal identification can allow us to discover new things about ourselves and increase awareness of our surroundings.

GUIDELINES FOR TRAINERS

Class members usually find most of the exercises in this chapter and Chapter 4 to be highly stimulating and motivating. You might want to capitalize on this interest and initiate several group discussions. Although most of the exercises and answers and comments are self-explanatory, a discussion can highlight the major points better. Moreover, some group members may be able to add new insights about learnings from some of the exercises.

When conducting these discussions, you might note that none of the exercises in this chapter is directly involved with idea generation. Instead, the major focus is upon sensing and understanding problems as well as the need to maintain a positive attitude. This emphasis is quite consistent with the notion that creativity and CPS involve more than just generating ideas.

Testing assumptions. The seven exercises in this section emphasize that we are conditioned to overlook major problem assumptions. The way we are educated and the experiences we've had tend to shape our behavior into a solution-minded mode of operation. However, as I noted previously in this chapter, we need to become more problem-minded. All of these exercises help demonstrate the importance of this need.

When discussing these exercises, you might note one paradox: The individual exercises are simplistic and appear to be relatively insignificant. However, they illustrate the high level of significance that should be placed upon testing all the assumptions we make about our problems. It is these assumptions that we use to circumscribe our problem boundaries and, in one sense, our minds. It really doesn't matter what type of problem is used to demonstrate the importance of testing assumptions. The objective is to have people experience the weaknesses in failing to test assumptions.

If your group doesn't seem to understand fully what you are trying to communicate, try another approach. Tell them to forget the exercises. Have them consider, instead, a problem that currently involves most of the group. Ask them to discuss different ways this problem can be defined and the assumptions used for each definition. Or, you simply might ask group members to share instances in which they later regretted not testing some problem assumptions.

Another way to emphasize the importance of this principle would be to use a group exercise. Split the class into two subgroups (no more than five to seven people per group). Have them go to separate rooms (or at least where they cannot hear the other group) and work on a problem that affects most class members.

Ask one group to spend 10 minutes discussing and analyzing the problem. In particular, tell them to examine all assumptions that might be made about the problem. Then, have them spend 15 minutes generating possible solutions.

Ask the other group to take a break while the first group is analyzing the problem. Once this time period is up, have the second group generate solutions for 15 minutes (at the same time as the first group), but without any discussion of the problem.

After both groups have finished, bring the groups together and have them share their ideas. All things being equal, the first group should have produced more creative ideas than the second group. In fact, there even is some indirect empirical research to support this expectation. Hackman and Morris (1975), for example, found that groups who discussed how to work on a task prior to idea generation generated ideas judged higher in creativity than groups who did not plan before generating ideas.

When discussing the individual exercises, people sometimes comment that a possible answer involves cheating. For example, if you use a circle to cut a pie, you are not doing it "correctly." However, you can point out that "correctness" in this case is relative, based upon a cultural assumption of how pies "should" be cut. The important learning from this exercise (as well as the others) is awareness of how self-imposed constraints can inhibit our creative thinking ability.

Of all the exercises that demonstrate the need to test assumptions, the nine-dot problem probably is the best known. It also seems to be a popular exercise in the academic problem solving literature. Most of this research tested the assumption that people have trouble solving the problem because of their tendency to fixate on the square shape of the dot pattern (e.g., Weisberg & Alba, 1981). The results of this research have been somewhat inconclusive and a little contradictory.

However, a recent experiment found that a solution can be achieved more easily once the problem is represented appropriately and a strategy developed (Lung & Dominowski, 1985). In particular, a key element seemed to be figuring out that lines do not have to begin and end on dots and that lines can intersect outside the square pattern. Learning the shape of the solution lines was found to be not so important, although it does affect ability to develop the "correct" solution. In general, subjects whose first two lines conformed to a square pattern were least likely to solve the problem. In addition, the presence of a center dot also seemed to make the problem more difficult to solve.

As I noted in the comments on the nine-dot problem, not everyone can solve this problem. You might note that these particular exercises are not designed to measure intelligence. No one should feel "stupid" if they cannot solve the nine-dot problem. This exercise and the others are intended solely to demonstrate general principles.

Positive attitude exercises. Exercises 6 and 7 obviously are similar in that both involve improving a product. However, more learning might be gained if you highlight the differences. In particular, point out how the flashlight exercise involves a known and accepted product; the golf cart design, in contrast, is relatively unknown and not accepted. As a result of this difference, people are likely to react more positively toward the flashlight than the golf cart. Thus, more learning may occur from comparing these two exercises than from examining either one alone.

An important thing to note about the golf cart exercise is that nothing was said in the instructions about making negative comments. I have used this exercise countless times and I have yet to encounter a group in which the majority of the comments were positive. The instructions were neutral, but most people redefine the task or respond negatively simply due to their conditioning.

After pointing out this tendency to stress the negative, you might ask them to discuss it. Ask them to recall what they were thinking at the time and why they responded the way they did. I have found that some people will carefully scrutinize the instructions again and look for a "loophole." They have that much trouble accepting that they thought of so many negative features.

A useful follow-up activity to this exercise is to have the class repeat the exercise or review their original comments. However, this time, ask them to take every negative feature they listed and convert it into a positive one. Some examples are provided in the answers and comment section.

When discussing this exercise, don't overstress the importance of looking for the positive. In the long run, it is more important to have a balanced view of new ideas. We need to be aware of both negative and positive features. However, the general slant should be positive, since your objective is to come up with something new. If you criticize everything negatively you never will accomplish anything.

Awareness exercises. Exercises 8 and 9 both involve patterns. However, there is one major difference. Exercise 8 (the addition exercise) is concerned with finding a pattern, while Exercise 9 (looking for commonality among numbers) involves avoiding a pattern. That is, successful performance on the addition exercise requires you to find and sustain the pattern that will lead to the correct answer. By comparison, searching for commonality among the numbers requires you to avoid a pattern in the sense that you must look for solutions other than the presumed "correct" one.

These patterns often operate as obstacles to creative thinking and problem solving. Our failure to become aware of how the situation around us is changing limits our ability to deal with it. This phenomenon frequently can be observed in cohesive groups. In such groups, an accepted behavior pattern develops and the group sticks to it no matter what the problem data may indicate—the so-called groupthink phenomenon (Janis, 1972).

We cannot always avoid being drawn into a patterned way of thinking. However, we should be aware that it is happening so we can try to break the pattern.

Sometimes patterns can be broken by disrupting the timing or pacing. In the addition exercise, you might mention that stopping momentarily to evaluate progress might help break the pattern. Another tactic might be to lump information together into more manageable units. Due to the mind's memory storage limitations, only so much information can be accommodated at any one time. Lumping or "chunking" information makes it easier to maintain a broader perspective on a problem. If we only have to consider a few bits of information at one time, we can better determine our overall problem solving progress.

For a dramatic effect, put the numbers on an overhead projector and present this exercise as a group effort. It is quite an experience to hear a number of people simultaneously add up simple numbers incorrectly!

When discussing Exercise 10 (describing your favorite room), there is at least one suggestion you might make. Mixed scanning usually will help most people recall large and easily noticeable objects in their rooms. However, it may have limited usefulness in increasing more general awareness about their rooms. You might suggest that people look for such things as differences and similarities in textures, temperatures, colors, size, function, shape, and so on. Then, you might have them compare these differences and similarities across categories. For instance, a textured, rectangular bedspread would contrast sharply with a smooth, oval-shaped wastebasket.

There also is one other suggestion I would add for doing Exercise 11 (pretending you are a particular object). After the class has completed this exercise, suggest that they examine how comfortable they were in doing it. Ask them to evaluate why something made them feel comfortable or uncomfortable. Then you might have them discuss any new insights gained that might help increase their problem solving effectiveness (or at least increase their awareness of problem situations).

SUMMARY

The creative thinking exercises in this chapter (Exercises 1 through 12) dealt with testing problem assumptions, looking for the positive features of ideas, and self- and problem-awareness. These exercises—and the ones that follow in Chapter 4—can help "warm up" our minds for creative problem solving. However, the exercises will not help unless we are committed to becoming more creative and expect to improve.

All the exercises in this chapter help demonstrate major creative thinking principles. The exercises that deal with testing problem assumptions are important, since the best ideas in the world will be of little value if the "wrong" problem is solved. The positive thinking exerises show that we need to make balanced evaluations of ideas (i.e., both positive and negative) and that we often can transform negative idea features into positive concepts. Finally, the exercises for increasing self- and problem-awareness illustrate the need to adopt a proper perspective when problem solving and to separate the relevant from the irrelevant.

Several guidelines for trainers also were discussed in this chapter. In general, it was suggested that trainers use group discussions to help clarify and identify implications of the exercises for CPS. In some instances, personal reports of experiences illustrating the principles can be helpful. For example, group members might talk about problems they experienced due to the incorrect assumptions they made.

Trainers also should make several specific points about the exercises. First, they should note that testing assumptions about problems helps avoid self-imposed problem solving constraints. The nine-dot problem is a case in point. Second, the positive thinking exercises help show that we need to overcome our conditioning to respond negatively to anything new. Finally, the awareness exercises help demonstrate the need to be aware of the patterns in problem solving. In particular, we need to create some patterns and break others in order to be successful problem solvers.

4
Creative Thinking Exercises: Part II

The exercises in this chapter (13 through 25) will help you practice the skills of fluency, flexibility, and originality. As in Chapter 3, a section on answers and comments follows presentation of the exercises.

In contrast to the exercises in Chapter 3, those in this chapter are more directly related to divergent generation processes. Whenever you generate any type of data during the CPS process, the quality of your data (and your solutions) will be enhanced if you have a high degree of fluency, flexibility, and originality.

FLUENCY EXERCISES

These exercises are concerned with your ability to generate a large amount of data with ease. A typical instance in which fluency would be helpful is the idea-finding stage of the CPS process. You might recall that idea-finding, like the other CPS stages, involves both divergent and convergent activities. During the divergent phase you need to generate lots of ideas. Of course, fluency also is important during divergence within the other stages of the CPS model.

Fluency is an important ability, since a large pool of information increases the odds of a high-quality outcome during the convergent stages of the CPS model. Thus, in idea-finding, an ability to generate a large number of ideas (without regard to their value) during the divergent phase will increase the probability that a high-quality idea will be chosen during the convergent phase.

Exercise 13. This exercise, invented by Bob McKim and described by

Adams (1979), works best with a group. However, it also can be modified for use by an individual.

For the group version, begin by assigning people to animals according to their last names. If their last names begin with A to E, they are sheep; if F to K, pigs; if L to R, cows; if S to Z, turkeys. Next, have each person find a partner (ideally, someone unknown) and look the partner in the eye. A leader should count to three, at which time everybody makes the sound—as loudly as possible—associated with his or her animal. If you don't happen to have a group of willing participants handy, select one of the animals and make its sound by yourself.

Exercise 14. In one minute, list as many words as you can that start with the letters "con."

Exercise 15. Write down as many ways you can think of that an egg and a book are similar. Then, write down ways that an egg, a book, and a windmill are similar.

Exercise 16. Write down at least five sentences containing five words each. Not so fast. It is not quite that easy. The first word of each sentence must begin with the letter C; the second word with the letter L; the third with I; the fourth with M; and the fifth with the letter B. That's right: CLIMB. Your sentences do not have to be entirely logical.

Exercise 17. One end of a string is tied to a doorknob. The other end is tied to the handle of a coffee cup so that the cup is suspended about two feet above the floor. How can you cut the string without the cup hitting the floor? You may not touch the cup or the string with your hands.

FLEXIBILITY EXERCISES

We usually think of someone who is physically flexible as being loose and able to move around easily. The same is pretty much true in regard to mental flexibility. As a creative thinking trait, flexibility involves the ability to generate different kinds of data. For instance, potential solutions for encouraging employees to report to work on time might be grouped as being: psychological (e.g., changing attitudes of individuals), social (e.g., using peer pressure), economic (e.g., financial rewards for showing up on time), and behavioral (e.g., using behavior modification techniques).

Another type of flexibility concerns the number of different approaches someone uses in dealing with problems. Obviously, someone who attempts to use the same approach for all types of problems is not very flexible. Sid Parnes tells a joke that effectively illustrates this point.

A patient told his psychiatrist that he (the patient) was dead. The psychiatrist decided that a simple experiment would demonstrate to the man that his belief was mistaken. The psychiatrist asked: "Do dead men bleed?" The man responded, "No" and the doctor immediately pricked the patient's

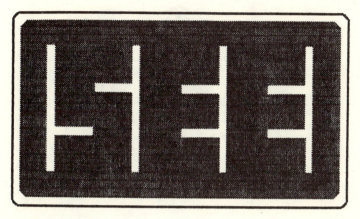

Figure 4–1
What Do You See?

finger. As the blood poured out of his wound, the patient exclaimed, "Well, I'll be darned. Dead men do bleed!"

As you might suspect, flexibility is somewhat related to fluency. In general, people who are highly fluent may not be very flexible. However, people who are highly flexible usually are minimally fluent (Glover, 1980). That is, you may have the ability to generate a lot of different ideas, but they may not all belong to different categories. On the other hand, someone who can generate many different categories and ideas within these categories must, by definition, also be fluent.

The following exercises are concerned with what might be called "approach" and "categorical" flexibility. Approach flexibility exercises (18, 19, and 20) use your ability to adopt different viewpoints when approaching a problem. The categorical flexibility exercises (21 and 22) focus upon your ability to generate many ideas within certain categories.

Exercise 18. Look at the illustration in Figure 4–1. What do you see?

Exercise 19. This exercise is very similar to the previous one. Look at the drawing in Figure 4–2. What do you see in this figure? What other perspectives might you adopt?

Exercise 20. Examine each picture (a, b, c, d, and e) in Figure 4–3. Which picture does not belong?

Exercise 21. Using no more than three categories, classify the following objects: (1) a drinking glass, (b) a telephone, (c) a stapler, (d) an automobile, (e) an elephant, and (f) flour. For example, you might describe how "a" and "b", "c" and "d", and "e" and "f", respectively, are similar. Next, try to organize the objects into two categories of three items each. Then, try one category.

Exercise 22. This is a classic problem solving exercise that originally was

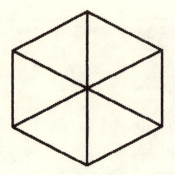

Figure 4–2
Cube Exercise

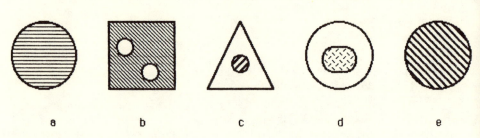

a   b   c   d   e

Figure 4–3
Which Figure Does Not Belong?

developed by Maier (1931). Assume that there are two strings attached to the ceiling of a room. The strings extend to within about one foot of the floor and are placed so that you cannot hold one string in one hand and reach the other. Your task is to tie the two strings together without removing them from the ceiling. You may use other items that you might find in a room of a house. If you can, try to think of more than one solution.

Hint: different solutions are based upon different categories of problem definitions. You might begin by considering how many different ways you can define this problem.

ORIGINALITY EXERCISES

Originality (defined as statistical infrequency) is closely related to and involved with creativity. According to several definitions, anything viewed as creative also is original. However, some people maintain that originality is useless unless the creative product also has some practical value (e.g., Perkins, 1981).

When thinking about originality, you might ask: "Original to whom?" (Of course, you might not be concerned with this. Instead, you might ask,

"Where are the exercises?") Most writers on the subject consider a product to be original if it is new to its creator. It does not necessarily have to be new to everyone outside the creator's field.

For example, you might invent a product that catches mice using cheese for bait and a spring-loaded metal bar that catches a mouse once the cheese is touched. You even might call your product a "mouse trap." If you are unfamiliar with other similar products, then your mouse trap is original to you. It's marketability and potential to be patented, of course, are entirely different matters.

We need to be original to be creative. The more original our ideas, the easier our problems will be to solve. However, don't worry if you are not as original as you would like. Not every idea you think of needs to be a better mouse trap.

Instead of worrying about originality when proposing ideas, you should be more concerned with generating a large number of ideas. Once you have really stretched your imagination and thought of every idea possible, originality usually will be taken care of.

The exercises that follow should help you experiment with your originality. The goal of these exercises is simply to allow you to practice being original. You are not expected to come up with "earth shaking" ideas. If you do, then congratulations; if you don't, then you still will have benefited from the experience of exercising your mind.

Exercise 23. Consider the possibilities if you could be in two places at the same time. What would happen? Who would be affected? Describe as many possibilities as you can think of.

Exercise 24. Using some or all of the following words as stimulators, design new household furniture products:

Pours	Vibrates
Cools	Solidifies
Mixes	Shakes
Beats	Vaporizes
Melts	Increases

Exercise 25. Write a short paragraph that uses only the words listed below. You may add only verbs, prepositions, and articles. Try to be as whimsical as possible.

Popsicle	Motorcycle	Television	Man
Boat	Helpful	Igloo	Haircut
Woman	Parking lot	Elephant	Weird

Candlelight	Jogging shoes	Composure	Ketchup
Wildlife	Reclined	Envelope	Airplane

EXERCISE ANSWERS AND COMMENTS

Exercise 13: On the surface, this exercise does not appear to have very much to do with fluency. From a psychological perspective, however, it is very related. A high level of fluency can involve a certain amount of risk taking. Since highly fluent people typically generate data without regard to their value, they may assume certain risks. For instance, some fluent people fear a loss of esteem in the eyes of others or self-esteem in wondering why they keep coming up with all those crazy ideas!

Exercise 14: This is an exercise in pure fluency. All you have to do is think of as many words as possible within the time limit. Although it may seem easy at first, you may find that the time limit throws a monkey wrench into the works. The one-minute deadline can create pressure that reduces your fluency. Fluency generally involves more than just generating data. To be truly fluent, you must be able to generate data fairly rapidly and often under time pressure.

Exercise 15: Exercise 14 dealt more with what might be described as "free association" fluency. That is, you generated as many words as possible with one often suggesting or leading to the next.

In contrast, this exercise requires you to use a somewhat different thinking process. You first must make a comparison between two or more objects, analyze the objects on the basis of this comparison, search for similarities, and then record your responses. Since there was no time limit imposed for this exercise, you probably didn't feel as much time pressure as in the previous exercise. Nevertheless, you still had the pressure of making analytical comparisons.

Some similarities between an egg and a book are that both: can be opened, can be used to prop up a window, can be opened flat, are associated with intellectuals (i.e., someone who reads a lot and an "egghead"), are used in cooking, have covers to protect their contents, and can be damaged if dropped from a height.

Similarities between an egg, a book, and a windmill might be a little more difficult to generate. Some possibilities are that all three: provide nourishment (a windmill irrigates crops; a book nourishes minds), can have living things inside of them (if the characters in a novel are "brought to life," aren't they living?), provide an income for some people, and involve movement of air (an egg yolk falling into a mixing bowl; the pages of a book being turned).

Exercise 16: If you could "climb" right into this exercise, you probably had little trouble coming up with four sentences. If you are highly fluent, you should be able to write such sentences without too much concentration. In fact, you should have felt that you could have written an unlimited number.

However, if you had trouble coming up with sentences, don't be too disappointed with yourself. Some people just need a little practice with their fluency. Or, you may have been trying too hard to develop "logical" sentences. As you can tell from the sample responses, not all the sentences need to make perfect sense:

Curb Limos In Master Bedrooms (a major problem)

Come Late In Mobster Bars (if you say so)

Catch Lizards in Mauve Baskets (the only color to use)

Cut Liver Into Micro-Bits (why not?)

Curse Lovers Inviting Many Bores (not me)

Exercise 17: This exercise, like the preceding ones, requires you to test the assumptions you make about general problem situations. Then, you need to discover that more than one solution is possible. In fact, the original developer of this exercise proposed only one correct solution. However, there are many possible ways to satisfy the conditions of this problem. To think of some of these possibilities, use visualization and be as fluent as you can.

The solution originally proposed as "correct" involved tying the string to the cup using a bow. If you cut the bow with a pair of scissors, the cup would not fall since it would remain tied to the string.

Some other possible solutions include: filling the room with gelatin (or foam or clay, or any other substance) so that the cup would not fall; placing a jet of air under the cup that would be strong enough to support it; removing the door from its hinges, gently setting the cup down on the floor, and cutting the string; holding the string with a pair of pliers (the instructions are to avoid touching the string with your hands) and cutting the string above the pliers; take the door, cup, and string to outer space where lack of gravity would prevent the cup from falling; and training an animal to hold the cup while you cut the string.

Exercises 18 and 19: A psychologist would note that Exercise 18 is concerned with figure-ground relationships. Depending upon your perspective, the gray and white colors in Figure 4–1 can alternate between the foreground and background. Thus, you might initially see what appears to be a sideview of bunk beds or broken goal posts. In this instance, white would be dominate and gray would be the background. However, you also can view the picture using gray as the foreground figure and white as the background. When you use this perspective, you should be able to see the block letters: "SEE."

One unique aspect of Figure 4–1 is that it illustrates how our minds allow us to only see one picture at a time in the figure. We either see "bunkbeds" or "SEE."

Exercise 19 is similar to Exercise 18 in that you are required to switch your perceptions. You might see either a cube or a six-sided figure made up of six triangles. Or, you might see a six-sided figure made up of two trapezoids containing three triangles each. Or, you might see three diamonds made up of two triangles. Or, you might see lots of other possibilities.

To be a flexible problem solver, you should be able to switch your perceptions of a problem fairly rapidly. Both of these exercises demonstrate how there usually is more than one way to view most situations appropriate for CPS.

Exercise 20: Did this exercise look familiar? If it did, you may be thinking of those dratted standardized tests many of us have taken. Or, it may have reminded you of an intelligence test. In either case, we usually assume that problems of this nature have only one correct answer. However, by adopting different viewpoints, you should be able to develop more than one "correct" answer.

Upon first examining the drawings in Figure 4–3, you might conclude that "d" is the one that doesn't belong. After all, it is the only one that has an inside oval-shaped figure. Then you might notice that "a" is the only one containing horizontal lines and "e" is the only large circle containing diagonal lines. And so forth. In fact, you even could note that all the figures belong since they all contain straight lines, they all contain curved lines, they all have open spaces inside, they all are of equal height, and they all are "needed" for top and side views of an architects rendering of a building and surrounding areas (e.g., "b" could be a top view of a building with skylights or heating equipment, "c" could be the side view of a second floor and roof, and "d" could be a top view of a swimming pool). If all of the drawings belong, then none of the drawings would not belong. Therefore, you might conclude that the problem can't be solved. (You probably can tell I didn't enjoy taking tests that involved problems such as these!)

Exercise 21: This exercise is concerned with categorical flexibility. It requires you to analyze the features of unrelated objects and determine how they might be similar. Then, you must organize the similarities to form logical categories. As a result, this exercise draws heavily upon both your divergent and convergent abilities.

A telephone and a drinking glass could form one category. Both of these items can be used for communication (an after-dinner speaker often will tap a glass with a spoon to get the attention of the others). A second category could be a stapler and flour since they both are used to bind together other things. Finally, a car and an elephant form a third category, since they both can be used for transportation.

Using these same six items, two categories also are possible. For instance, a car, stapler, and telephone are similar since they all can involve queues or waiting in line. Cars line up for gas, staples are lined up in a stapler, and telephone calls often are "lined up" waiting for available lines. The remaining three items—a drinking glass, an elephant, and flour—are similar in that they all involve pouring.

Exercise 22: Maier (1970) suggests four different categories of solutions for this problem. Each category is determined by how you perceive the problem.

First, if you perceive the problem as having arms that are too short, your solutions might involve ways to extend your reach. For example, you might try using a stick to pull the other string toward you. A second category is based upon the assumption that the strings are too short. Possible solutions in this case could involve ways to lengthen one of the strings. You might tie another string (or something like a drapery cord) to one of the strings, thus making it possible to tie together both. Third, you might define your problem as how to make one string remain in place while you reach for the other. One solution would be to tie down or weight one of the strings. Finally, a fourth category of solutions might involve a problem of how to get one string to come to you while you hold on to the other. To do this, you might use a fan to blow one string to you or tie a small weight to a string and swing it until you can reach it.

Exercise 23: The two words "What if?" probably have led to the development of many novel ideas and products. By posing this simple, open-ended question, your mind can be opened up to consider many different possibilities.

Some responses to the question are: you could accomplish twice as much work (or play); you could commit numerous crimes and always have an alibi (at least until you were caught in both places); if you made a mistake, you could blame it on your other self; when family functions are scheduled at the same time as your favorite sporting event, you could attend both; you would only have to exercise (or do anything distasteful) half as much; if you sometimes were lonely, you could call yourself on the telephone and have a chat; and you could have an affair without your spouse wondering why you work late so much.

Exercise 24: As you know, it is not always easy to be fluent when generating ideas. The "well" often runs dry after so much time. To overcome this difficulty, many people find it helpful to use various types of stimulation. Random words often work very well in this regard. By relating random words to a problem area, many new ideas can be prompted.

There are several ways you can do this. First, you can look at each word and write down whatever product might be suggested. Or, you can combine two of the words in the order listed (or in reverse order).

When thinking of your products, remember that you need to defer criticism. If you initially think of an impractical or "stupid" idea, try to modify it and make it more practical. Here are some examples.

Beats—design a sofa that has built-in beaters to keep off dust. This is a little impractical. However, maybe a couch could emit ultrasonic sound waves that would "vibrate" (another of the stimulator words) away any falling dust.

Vaporizes—install a humidifier/dehumidifier inside a sofa or large chair. Or, develop a live plant arrangement that has its own miniature rain forest.

Melts-Shakes—design table legs so that if they begin to wobble on an uneven surface, the bottom of the leg melts and conforms to the shape of the floor.

Pours-Solidifies—develop pre-cast tables and chairs by pouring (another of the words) a mixture that hardens in a form.

Increases-Cools—design a line of air-conditioned (or heated) furniture that also is resistant to perspiration. Or, design a chair that responds to your body temperature, cooling when you heat up and vice versa.

Exercise 25: In addition to being a test of your originality, this exercise also tests your ability to rapidly process many bits of organization and organize it in some meaningful way (O.K., perhaps in a semi-meaningful way). Unless you believe that monkeys using typewriters could randomly produce all of Shakespeare's works, your paragraph should be unique and original to just you. After you have finished writing it, look it over and see if there is some sense of continuity. It can be difficult to achieve a sense of flow when you are limited by available data. If you would like an even greater challenge of your creativity, try writing a paragraph that uses the words in the order they are presented.

Because I do not feel the need for a major challenge, the following example uses the words in a random order:

A man saw a woman with jogging shoes eat a popsicle. To be helpful, he gave her an envelope to put it in. She reclined on her motorcycle in the parking lot and asked, "Want a haircut on television?" They took a boat to an airplane and ate elephant with ketchup by candlelight. He learned she lived with weird wildlife in an igloo. He lost his composure.

GUIDELINES FOR TRAINERS

In the beginning of this chapter, I briefly discussed the importance of fluency. I noted that there is a positive relationship between the number of ideas generated and idea quality. That is, the more ideas you generate, the greater the odds that at least one will be capable of resolving your problem. If necessary, you might further illustrate this point using something like the following example.

Assume that there are eight high-quality ideas out of 400 for resolving some problem. That is, out of a possible 400 ideas, eight have the best probability of actually resolving your problem. If you spend your time generating one idea, evaluating it, accepting or rejecting it, generating another idea, and so forth, you will use up a lot of time trying to uncover all eight high-quality ideas. Unless you have unlimited time, you never may uncover even one of the high-quality solutions. Therefore, the only "logical" approach is to generate as many ideas as you can think of and then evaluate them.

Incidentally, all of this was put much more simply by Alex Osborn (1963) who emphasized the principle: "Quantity breeds quality." What you put forth in quantity, you will get back in quality.

Most of the exercise answers and comments in this chapter are fairly clear-cut. There are a few instances, however, where you might want to clarify the implications for CPS. For instance, in Exercise 18 ("What do you see?"), you might have the class play around with it a little more. Ask them to practice switching their perceptions rapidly. Tell them to look at the "bunkbed" designs, then look at the word "SEE," then the bunkbeds, and so forth. Do this until everyone can switch back and forth easily.

Next, ask them to experiment with a "real" problem. You might have them assume the role of a production manager who is notified that there is excessive scrap waste. What other ways might you redefine this problem? For example, you might redefine it as: In what ways might we encourage employees to conserve material? Be more efficient? Use materials that won't produce as much waste? Use less wasteful patterns? If the group thinks of enough redefinitions, one of them might lead directly to a solution. When this occurs, you have a combination problem and solution—a "problution" (VanGundy, 1986).

The only other suggestion I have for using the exercises in this chapter is to try doing them in groups. Have the groups work separately on selected exercises and then share their results with the total group. Their motivation for doing the exercises is likely to be higher if they can share their reactions and ideas with others.

The following guidelines for fluency, flexibility, and originality might help some people with the exercises. You could discuss them with your class before they do the exercises. Or, you might experiment and discuss the guidelines with only one-half of the class members. Then, have everyone do the exercises and see if discussing the guidelines first for half the class seemed to make any difference in their performance. Of course, it will be difficult to measure performance objectively for many of the exercises. Nevertheless, even rough assessments should prove interesting.

General guidelines.

1. The most important of all the guidelines is to defer judgment. Encourage the class to turn off the self-criticism they normally use when

problem solving. The quantity and quality of their solutions are likely to be much higher if they minimize criticism.

2. Stress the importance of maintaining a positive attitude. The exercises should be approached with the attitude that every one can be solved or performed satisfactorily.

3. If you plan to do the exercises as a group, you might encounter a low level of participation. This often happens when a group is relatively new, there are major status differences within the group, severe interpersonal conflicts exist, or several members are shy. If participation appears to be a problem, don't force it at the outset. Instead, have class members work some of the exercises alone in small groups and then pass their written responses to other members. Sometimes, this approach will help loosen up people and establish enough trust so that a total group discussion can be conducted.

4. If group members are comfortable with it, you might suggest that they use a relaxation technique before doing some of the exercises. One simple relaxation method is to lie down and alternately tense and relax different muscle groups. Begin with the toes and work up the body. Another method is to focus upon breathing. Have the class relax as much as possible and then practice breathing in through their noses and exhaling through their mouths. Tell them to try and experience their breathing and develop control over it. One of many resources for relaxation techniques is *The Relaxation & Stress Reduction Workbook* by Davis, McKay, and Eshelman (1980).

Fluency guidelines.

• Let your mind run free. Try to free your thinking from any restraints. Put aside whatever else you might be thinking or worrying about at the time. Write down whatever pops into your head.

• Don't be afraid to write down anything you think of. Whatever ideas you come up with should be written down. You always can come back later and evaluate your thoughts. Give the censor in your mind a "pink slip."

• Try using free association. As soon as you think of one idea, use it as a stimulus for the next one. Then, use this idea as a stimulus and continue the process until you have exhausted all ideas you can think of. For example, the word "roof" might suggest the word "house" which, in turn, might suggest "live in," and so on.

• Look for idea stimulation in your immediate environment. A clock on the wall, a table, or a lamp, for instance, all might suggest a variety of approaches to use for solving a problem. Look for the basic concepts or principles involved in the objects that surround you. In addition to illumination, a lamp also generates heat which warms up people and things.

Does that suggest a new or different viewpoint? Try using other objects in the same way.

• Be aware of the sometimes dangerous trade-offs involved when striving for a high level of fluency. Sometimes you may sacrifice solution quality for quantity of potential solutions (Perkins, 1981). For example, generating a large number of ideas consumes time. If you have only limited time, you may not be able to generate every possible idea you can think of. Instead, you may need to restrict yourself using a deadline or quota of ideas.

Flexibility guidelines.

• Experiment with different problem solving languages. For example, if a mathematical approach doesn't seem to work, try solving the problem visually. Or, if visual problem solving doesn't do the trick, try sketching the problem. Verbal problem solving is another approach. Discuss the problem with someone else or don't be afraid to discuss it out loud with yourself.

• Try generating solutions using each of the five senses of seeing, touching, hearing, smelling, and tasting. As an example, consider the exercise involving classification of a drinking glass, a telephone, or an elephant (Exercise 21). One approach to this exercise would be to think of how each item looks, feels, sounds, smells, and tastes. These similarities (and differences) then might form the basis for a variety of classification schemes.

• Break down the problem into different kinds of things, parts, shapes, operations, purposes, functions (roles played by parts), phases, values, or forms. Then, try to generate as many ideas as possible for each area. An excellent reference on classification is *Creative Analysis* by Upton, Samson, and Farmer (1978).

Exercise 20 (deciding upon the drawing that doesn't belong) might be dealt with easily using this guideline. Beyond the obvious categories of parts and shapes, you might experiment with the not-so-obvious ones such as operations or functions. Thus, you might visualize how different shapes might move and affect other parts. Some parts might affect others in the same way, while some might have a unique effect (e.g., circles would have one type of effect when rotated and triangles would have a totally different effect).

Originality guidelines.

• Don't try too hard to be original. If you overemphasize originality, you may place too much stress upon yourself and inhibit your originality. Allow your ideas to flow and constantly be alert for new ways of viewing your problems and solving them. If you try too hard, you may reduce the number of ideas you generate and thus restrict solution quality (Stein, 1975).

• Recognize and accept your own worth and value as a creative individual. If you sincerely believe you are creative, it will be easier for you to develop unique ideas.

• Tell yourself to be original. (As a trainer, you can instruct participants to be original.) There is some research evidence that instructing people to be original is more likely to result in high originality (e.g., Maltzman, Bogartz & Berger, 1958). The results, however, are far from conclusive.

• Use a variety of different stimuli to help suggest ideas. For the problem of what would happen if you could be in two places at the same time (Exercise 23), different stimuli could suggest many possibilities. For instance, using a telephone as a stimulus could lead to many ideas based upon various forms of communication.

SUMMARY

The exercises in this chapter deal with the creative abilities of fluency, flexibility, and originality. Fluency involves the ability to generate a large amount of data rapidly. In general, the more problem data you generate, the higher will be the quality of your final solution. Flexibility, a close relative of fluency, can be classified as being either "approach" or "categorical." "Approach" flexibility is the ability to use many different approaches and viewpoints when trying to solve a problem. "Categorical" flexibility involves the ability to generate many different types of problem data.

In working with groups using the exercises in this chapter, trainers should: emphasize the relationship between idea quantity and quality, help the groups examine implications of the exercises for CPS, and experiment with different methods for groups to use the exercises.

Some guidelines for being fluent, flexible, and original include: defer all criticism when generating data, maintain a positive attitude, use silent, written procedures in groups in which participation initially is low, experiment with different relaxation techniques, try using free association and environmental stimuli when striving for fluency, experiment with different problem solving languages, use all your senses and break down problems when trying to increase flexibility, avoid trying too hard, recognize and accept your own creative worth, and use a variety of stimuli to help increase originality.

5
Description of the CPS Process

A brief overview of the CPS model was presented in Chapter 1. A similar overview will be used in this chapter, but more detail will be provided. The major principles involved in using the model also will be highlighted in this chapter. And, special consideration will be given to some fundamental "rules of thumb" for divergent and convergent activities within each stage.

OVERVIEW OF THE CPS MODEL

As mentioned in Chapter 1, the CPS model contains six major stages: objective-finding, fact-finding, problem-finding, idea-finding, solution-finding, and acceptance-finding. The first three stages are concerned primarily with understanding and choosing a challenge. Idea-finding is used to generate potential solutions, solution-finding involves deciding upon the best solution, and a major focus of acceptance-finding is solution implementation.

Not all of the stages will be needed for every problem or challenge you face. Sometimes you can skip the first three stages, for example, and begin generating ideas. Other times, however, you might need to use all six stages. It all depends upon how familiar you are with your problem "mess."

I also should note that the model is designed to be flexible. It was not designed as a rigid, sequential process in which you must start with point X and proceed directly to point Y. Instead, you should feel free to leave one stage at any time and return to a previous stage or move on to a new stage. As long as you keep your primary objective in view, the way you get there is not all that important.

For instance, you might decide you need to recycle to fact-finding after completing problem-finding. Such a decision usually occurs when you notice that you do not have enough information to choose a challenge. Or, as another example, you might notice during idea-finding that you are generating ideas for a problem different from the one you originally had chosen at the end of problem-finding. In this instance, you should recycle to problem-finding and explore additional problem definitions.

You also shouldn't be surprised to be in acceptance-finding and discover you still don't clearly understand the problem. Even after working through all the previous stages, you may be about to implement a solution and decide that you need more information. Or, new information may become available that causes you to reevaluate your perceptions of the problem. For example, I have been in many groups in which a new member joins and influences the others to revise their problem perceptions.

If you ever decide to leave one stage of the model and return to a previous one, be certain that enough time is available for "backtracking." This is especially important if you are not certain about the need to recycle. Searching for new information consumes time that may or may not lead to the desired payoff. Therefore, you must weigh the costs of any information search against the expectation that the outcome of the search will help you solve the problem. In other words, don't spin your wheels trying to solve a problem that no longer can be solved.

Another major variable involved in any decision to recycle is perceived problem importance. Most of your problems vary in their importance to you, depending upon your particular values and needs. In addition, some problems may assume special importance to you if your boss "encourages" (and I use the word loosely!) you to deal with them. Therefore, when you think you need to recycle, you must decide if the problem's importance justifies the effort involved.

A brief description of each of the six CPS stages is presented next. A more detailed discussion of the stages, as well as techniques to facilitate the activities involved in each, can be found in Chapters 6 through 13.

Objective-Finding (Chapter 6). The model begins with awareness and recognition of various concerns, challenges, and opportunities in your life. Sometimes these factors are fairly well known to you; at other times, you may have only a vague notion as to what areas need attention. The objective-finding stage will help you clarify several potential starting points and select one primary objective to focus your efforts.

Fact-Finding (Chapter 7). The primary purpose of this stage is to increase your understanding of the target area you have selected. To do this, you will be instructed how to gather as much relevant data as possible about your concern, challenge, or opportunity. As you explore the features and dimensions of your objectives, certain bits of information should emerge as being most relevant to you. By analyzing this information and sorting the relevant from the irrelevant, an initial problem definition may materialize. You then can use this definition (or your awareness of a more specific target area) as the starting point for the next stage.

Problem-Finding (Chapter 8). When you finish this stage, you should have selected the one problem statement (or a cluster of related statements) that best captures your concern, challenge, or opportunity area. To do this, you first will examine all the relevant information you generated in the previous stage. Then, you will develop a number of different problem statements. Of these statements, at least one should appear to have the potential for stimulating a variety of potential solutions.

Idea-Finding (Chapters 9 and 10). You will begin this stage by generating as many potential solutions (ideas) as you can for your problem. Several different techniques will be suggested to help you do this individually (Chapter 9) as well as in group situations (Chapter 10). At the end of this stage, you will narrow your idea list and select those with the highest potential for resolving your problem.

Solution-Finding (Chapter 11). This stage of the process will help you systematically analyze your potential solutions and select the best ones for possible implementation. You first will be asked to generate a list of criteria to use in idea evaluation. Then, you will use the most important criteria to judge your ideas. Finally, you will choose one or more solutions that you think have the highest potential to resolve your problem.

Acceptance-Finding (Chapter 12). The last stage of the CPS model involves considering ways to overcome all the obstacles that might prevent you from applying your solution (or solutions) and then developing an action plan to guide implementation. Rather than just hoping for the best when implementing a solution, this stage forces you to analyze all the factors that could contribute to successful implementation. After all, the best solution in the world won't help if you can't use it!

The six stages of the CPS model are concerned with both divergent and convergent activities. Each stage starts with a divergent search for some type of data (e.g., facts, problems, ideas, criteria, obstacles). During this portion of each stage, you should "stretch" your thinking to gather as much data as you can. The second half of each stage is devoted to a convergent narrowing down of whatever data you collected. In this half, you must choose from the data you generated during the divergent phase.

The CPS model involves basic cycles of diverging-converging, diverging-converging, and so forth until the problem is resolved. One primary reason for these cycles is to keep you on course when problem solving. If you used only divergent activities, you probably would not achieve any sense of closure; if you used only convergent activities, the overemphasis upon judgment would lead to few, if any, creative solutions.

PRINCIPLES FOR DIVERGING AND CONVERGING

The principles presented in this section should help you make better use of the CPS process. If you study them carefully and try to incorporate them into your "tool kit" of problem solving behaviors, your problems will be easier to solve and you should be happier with the outcome.

However, achieving this goal may not be easy. Simply reading about the stages of the model and some basic principles will not be enough. Instead, you must practice using the model and the principles as much as you can. Direct experience is the only way to become proficient with the model.

The divergent and convergent principles that follow are drawn from the work of Isaksen and Treffinger (1985).

Divergent principles. These principles should help you increase the amount of data you can generate within the first portion of each stage.

1. Defer judgment. If you ignore all of the other principles of divergence, remember this one! It probably is the most important one. When generating data for any of the CPS stages, you should try to withhold all evaluation. Because judging seems to be such a natural behavior, it can be difficult to defer. However, it is essential for improving the quality of your problem solving. Just keep telling yourself (or gently reminding others in a group setting) that judgment will come later.

Another thing to remember about deferring judgment is that evaluation can be both positive and negative. It sometimes can be just as harmful to make an untimely positive evaluation as a negative one. For example, you might train yourself to stop commenting on how terrible someone's idea is as soon as you see it. However, if you also loudly exclaim how wonderful an idea is upon first hearing it, you would be just as guilty of violating this principle.

2. Think of as many ideas as you can. Really push yourself to seek quantity of data. Regardless of which stage you are in, quality isn't very important during divergence. Quality assumes importance during the convergent portion of each stage, especially during solution-finding and acceptance-finding. Whenever you are diverging, purge your mind of whatever idea pops up and write it down. Then, after you have listed all possible ideas, you can evaluate them and look for quality.

3. Be receptive to all ideas. Whether generated by yourself or someone else, you should try to accept every idea proposed. No matter how silly or outrageous an idea might appear when first mentioned, you might be able to transform it into something more workable. However, if you reject such

ideas outright, you never will have the opportunity to explore their potential.

When I conduct workshops, I often try to illustrate this principle using an analogy involving flowers and weeds. Suppose I am holding a bunch of seeds in one hand. I examine the seeds and give the ones that don't appeal to me to my friend Eleanor. Then, I plant the remaining seeds and wait for them to grow. Once fully grown, I discover that I have produced a healthy crop of weeds. Meanwhile, Eleanor has planted her seeds and produced a beautiful flower garden.

We often respond to new ideas in a similar way. We immediately reject the ones that don't appeal to us and retain only those with immediate appeal. The others we reject. However, by discarding ideas prematurely, we frequently lose many ideas with the potential to resolve our problems. Ideas are not just the raw data we transform into solutions; ideas also are stimuli that we can use to generate new and perhaps better ideas.

4. Push to diverge as much as possible. If you ever have participated in any form of athletic training, you know there is a limit to how much you can do. Each of us only can run so fast, swim so far, or jump so high. However, we rarely achieve our full potential. To do so requires that we push ourselves and then push some more. The same holds true when generating data.

It often is easy to stop diverging when we think we have thought of everything possible. If this happens to you frequently, tell yourself that you are capable of generating more. Take a break and relax or work on something else. Then, resume diverging and try for as much data as you can. Another way to "stretch" your mind is to look around for different stimuli. For instance, what data might be suggested by a picture on the wall or a light that flickers on and off?

5. Allow ideas to "incubate." Be a "chicken" and "sit" on your ideas for awhile. Don't assume that all the ideas you possess are the ones you can think of at any one time. Take a "vacation" from your problem and do something different. Then, return and see if you can modify the ideas you thought of previously or generate new ones. Because we often think of ideas when we are doing something else, you also might want to keep a small notepad handy to jot down ideas that pop into your head.

6. Look for ways to modify or otherwise combine ideas. An idea that initially appears to be impractical often can be improved drastically by a simple modification. By altering a shape, function, process, or other aspect of an idea, it often is possible to produce an innovative solution. For instance, an idea for an ordinary table lamp might be improved by adding a device so the lamp also can serve as a secondary heat source (cats would find such a feature especially appealing).

You also should search for ways to combine different ideas. In the vernacular of CPS, this is known as "hitchhiking" or "piggybacking." Take one idea and improve upon it by adding some or all of the features of another. When groups are diverging, hitchhiking is quite common and should be encouraged. In a group, you should try to use other ideas as springboards for new ideas.

Convergent principles. During the second half of each CPS stage, you need to become analytical and reduce the amount of data you generated during the first half. That is, you need to converge and select the best possible outcome for each stage. The six principles that follow should help you do this.

1. Be systematic. Contrary to what many people think, CPS involves more than just diverging and "free wheel" thinking. As I have noted previously, there is an analytical component to the process that requires you to be systematic and efficient. When you are trying to sort out the data you generated during divergence, you should develop a plan. In particular, you should try to be as systematic as possible to help you decide which bits of data are most important to you. For example, you might want to group data into logical categories and then evaluate the data within each group using various criteria.

2. Clarify and make known your evaluation criteria. We all make decisions every day using criteria. We have certain standards that help us choose from among different alternatives. For most of our decisions, these criteria are implicit. In many cases, we are not even aware of the criteria we are using.

There is nothing wrong with using implicit criteria. We usually can get by with little trouble and still solve many problems. However, difficulties develop when dealing with important problems or in group situations. In either case, you should try to make your criteria as explicit as possible. When converging by yourself, take a few minutes to reflect upon what is important to you in regard to the problem you are trying to resolve; when working in a group, let others know what decision-making factors are important to you. If everyone does this, there will be less conflict and agreement will be achieved more easily.

3. Avoid premature closure on data. The purpose of converging is to achieve closure on data generated during the diverging phase. However, we sometimes do this too quickly. It is easy to "settle" upon several ideas, for example, that initially appear to have solution potential. Converging too fast may cause you to overlook new data. Instead of trying for immediate closure, review the data for anything unusual that might be modified or suggest a different approach. Do this at any time during the converging process. Then, if you think of new data, add them to the list you already generated and continue converging.

4. Be realistic about your problem. We all have to deal with many unpleasant things in life. In most cases, the best way to deal with such situations

is to face them head on—confront them and deal with them as well as we can. Putting off such encounters often will make matters worse.

The same philosophy applies to the CPS process. Many of our problems contain unpleasant features we try to avoid. However, hoping that these unpleasant things will go away rarely works. Some unpleasant matters do take care of themselves over time, but the majority probably get worse.

When you converge during CPS, evaluate all the features of your problem to make sure you are not consciously or subconsciously avoiding anything. It is better to deal with such matters now than wait for the last stage of the model when it might be too late to do anything. Take a little time to anticipate some major difficulties you might face in dealing with the problem in the future. Make any adjustments you need to (or can make) now. Then, put aside a list of potential problems you might need to consider during acceptance-finding.

5. Avoid the "killer instinct" when evaluating data. Some people seem to have a pent-up desire to tear apart all new ideas. Even if they defer judgment when diverging, they often pull all stops as soon as they begin converging. It's almost as if they think: "O.K., I did what you asked during divergence, and now it's my turn to really let loose and cut up all the ideas!"

As I mentioned before, criticism can be both positive and negative. A balanced approach usually will prove beneficial during any type of evaluation. It is especially important when converging within the CPS process.

If you want to do an unbalanced evaluation, tilt your evaluation more toward the positive. Instead of viewing your task as getting rid of unworthy ideas, redefine your objective as developing positive aspects of all the ideas. Then, use those positive features to help converge upon new potential solutions.

6. Don't lose sight of where you are going. There is an old saying that: "If you don't know where you're going, you'll never get there." When you analyze and revise data during convergence, keep in mind why you are using the CPS process. Don't get so involved in the details of the process that you forget about the "big picture."

CPS is intended to help you explore and deal with the concerns, challenges, and opportunities you face in life. It is not intended as a panacea for all your problems or just another way to make life more confusing. Use CPS as it best suits you, but don't let it use you.

GUIDELINES FOR TRAINERS

Perhaps the best way to help people learn about the CPS process is for them to experience it. To do this, you might try using mixed groups of experienced and inexperienced CPS users. Obviously, you can't do this if everyone is inexperienced. However, once you have trained a small group, you can use them in subsequent training sessions.

I recently participated in a "think tank" type of meeting in which I was able to observe the benefits of mixing different levels of CPS experience (Gilinsky, 1985). The purpose of the meeting was to brainstorm a variety of creative projects we might work on together (e.g., films, books, training materials, conference centers). About two-thirds of the participants were experienced in using CPS. The rest worked in various "creative" occupations such as slide show productions and scriptwriting.

Although it was not intentional, we divided ourselves into small groups so that each group had a combination of experienced and inexperienced CPS users. At first, some of the inexperienced users held back while they observed the rest of us in action (most of us experienced users also knew each other from previous interactions). Eventually, the inexperienced users joined in and made many valuable contributions.

It was particularly interesting to note how the inexperienced members began to model some of the problem solving behaviors of the more experienced members. For instance, most experienced members took the lead in generating a variety of ideas without regard to their quality. The other members soon picked up on this principle and tried to follow suit.

The overall playful attitude of most of the experienced members also helped produce a climate conducive for creative participation by the inexperienced users. I believe that most of them learned that their ideas initially would be accepted without criticism. (To be accurate, I should note that even the experienced users violated this principle on occasion.)

One outcome of this meeting was that the inexperienced users were able to "learn on the job." As a result, our next meeting should proceed more smoothly. Participation should be higher and it should be easier to begin converging.

Overview of the model. When presenting an overview of the model, emphasize the model's flexibility. Many people lose interest in the CPS process when they incorrectly conclude they must use all six stages every time they have a problem to solve. Also be sure to note that users should feel free to leave any stage and move to another one.

If you have the time, you might want to discuss some of the factors involved in making a decision to recycle to a previous stage or skip ahead to another stage. Usually, such decisions arise when there is insufficient or inadequate information (as perceived by the problem solver). The two most important factors seem to be the amount of perceived time available and problem importance.

Time obviously is a major variable, since backtracking will consume time and moving forward will save time. In both cases, the costs of making such moves will need to be weighed carefully.

You also might stress that time can be both subjective and objective. It all depends upon the constraints of the situation and any self-imposed constraints. That is, time can be objective if you know that a problem absolutely must be solved within a specified time period—for example, your boss asks you to complete a task no later than yesterday! On the other hand, time can be more subjective if you place time constraints upon yourself that really do not exist. You may want to get a problem "out of the way," for instance, but it is not really critical to resolution that you do so.

Deciding upon a problem's importance can be especially messy when working in groups. Conflicts in values, needs, and general problem perceptions make it difficult to achieve consensus. To help a group achieve consensus, there are several tactics you can use. For instance, have the group list different problem viewpoints. Then, select two viewpoints and ask them to combine them into one way of viewing the general problem situation.

As an example, suppose that a group is given the task of devising ways to improve customer service. Some group members might believe that the central problem is to encourage more employees to participate in voluntary customer relations training. Others might believe that the problem is having more on-site visits by higher management. Combining these two viewpoints might result in a redefined problem of convincing upper management to require customer relations training.

When discussing recycling to a previous stage, you could note that a curvilinear relationship might exist between perceived problem importance and difficulty of the decision to recycle. Put another way, a recycling decision should be relatively easy for problems low and high in importance and relatively difficult for moderately important problems.

Thus, when a problem is seen as low or high in importance, it will be relatively easy to decide upon the desirability of recycling. If a problem is not important, then recycling may not be worth the effort; if a problem is seen as very important, then recycling easily would be justified to increase the odds of resolving the problem. However, recycling decisions will be more difficult when a problem is perceived to be only moderate in importance. For such problems, you will have to weigh how much effort you are willing to expend when the problem is not quite so important to you.

Allow me to give you a somewhat exaggerated example. Suppose you are watching TV in the living room of your house. Your daughter runs in shouting excitedly, "The house is on fire!" Unless you have a perverse "thing" about fires or you desperately need the insurance money, you probably would consider this situation to be an important problem. As a result, it would be easy for you to decide that action is required. It would be well worth any effort you might expend to find out if the house really is on fire.

On the other hand, another daughter might run in during the climax of your favorite TV show and tell you that the cat did a "no no" again in your bedroom closet. In this case, you might not view the problem as important enough to justify leaving your show. Some things just have to wait.

Principles of divergence and convergence. Talking about these principles is not likely to lead to as much understanding as practicing with them. If time is available, I would suggest that you have your class work on some problems to help illustrate these principles.

Before discussing the principles, consider having groups work together in solving some problem that is relevant to most members. Next, have them discuss what principles of divergence and convergence they seemed to follow and which they violated. Also, have them note which ones they consider to be most important. Then, have them select another problem and try to pay closer attention to the principles. Even though the process may be disrupted somewhat in doing this, make sure they evaluate their ongoing divergent and convergent behavior. Eventually, they should become more aware of the impact their behaviors can have upon the CPS process.

Incidentally, there is a dramatic way to emphasize the importance of deferred judgment. I first learned of this from Eugene Irving, a professor and creativity trainer from Illinois. Have the class pound their fists on their tables and chant in unison with you: "No evaluation with ideation!" Repeat this four or five times. They will begin to get the idea (either that, or they will start a riot).

SUMMARY

The CPS process involves six interrelated stages: objective-finding, fact-finding, problem-finding, idea-finding, solution-finding, and acceptance-finding. Sometimes you will want to use all six stages and other times one or two stages will do—it all depends upon how vague your problem is to you.

When using the CPS model, be flexible within the stages. Depending upon how comfortable you are with problem information at any one time, you may want to skip ahead to another stage or recycle backward to a previous stage. If you decide to skip a stage or return to a previous one, be sure to weigh how much time you have and the importance of the problem to you.

Each stage of the CPS process is designed to serve a specific function. However, all the stages are alike in that each begins with a divergent phase and ends with a convergent phase.

Objective-finding begins with a search for concerns, challenges, and opportunities and ends with selection of an area in which to focus your efforts. Fact-finding helps you search for relevant problem information and narrow down this information as an initial definition begins to emerge. Problem-finding, the third stage, assists you in looking at your problem from many different perspectives and choosing one with the highest potential for generating solutions. Idea-finding guides you in generating a variety of potential solutions and sorting through these to select the best ones. The fifth stage, solution-finding, allows you to analyze your potential solutions in a systematic manner and choose those with the highest potential for resolving your problem. Finally, acceptance-finding begins with consideration of all implementation obstacles and it ends with development of an action plan that will help ensure successful problem resolution.

Major divergent principles include: defer judgment, think of as many ideas as you can, be receptive to all ideas, push to diverge as much as possible, allow ideas to "incubate," and look for ways to modify or otherwise combine ideas. Some major principles of convergence are: be systematic, clarify and make known your evaluation criteria, avoid premature closure on data, be realistic about your problem, avoid the "killer instinct" when evaluating ideas, and don't lose sight of where you are going.

Some guidelines for trainers to consider are: mix together experienced and inexperienced CPS users to help the inexperienced users learn the CPS process and use group problem solving experiences to help illustrate principles of divergence and convergence.

6
Objective-Finding

You are walking in an open swamp surrounded by a dense forest. Everything is the color gray. As you trudge along, your nostrils flare from the acrid smell that wafts upward from the gooey swamp mud and water. Strange sounds can be heard from the dark forest. You are tired from walking all day. Worst of all, you are lost. You think you are walking in the direction you want to be, but you're not sure.

You spot a tree stump and sit down to rest and get your bearings. To your left, you notice what might be the opening for a trail through the forest. The rest of the forest surrounding the swamp looks the same. A small airplane flies high above, almost out of view.

While swigging down some of the putrid, foul-tasting water in your flask, the forest to your right suddenly erupts into a cacophonous symphony of sounds. You remove your dictionary from your backpack.

As soon as you return your dictionary, you notice that the harsh-sounding symphony from your right has intensified. The sounds now seem to be moving toward you. There is apparent movement from the same place in the forest. And the movement seems to be coming toward you. You barely notice the acrid smell wafting toward your flared nostrils. However, your senses of sight and hearing are heightened.

Without giving it any thought, you start running toward the forest opening at your left. It is not the direction you were going before you stopped to rest. However, something tells you to veer left.

You plod along, knees lifting high to avoid tripping over the unknown. The sound behind you now grows steadily louder and increases in intensity. Then, without warning, a rhythmic beating begins. Although not as cacophonous as the original sound, the beating is quite noticeable and harsh.

You reach the opening in the forest and rush down the path before you. As you turn to face the sound, you trip over a tree root. Lying on the ground, you notice that the candy bar in your front shirt pocket is smashed beyond recognition. Picking yourself up, you resume running.

The noise seems to remain the same distance behind you, no matter how fast or slow you run. Suddenly, you have the sensation of falling. Quickly looking around, you immediately know why you have this sensation: You are falling. You are falling into a pit.

After brushing yourself off, you remove the pieces of the crushed "lucky porcelain figurine" you always carry in your rear pants pocket. Looking around, you notice that the walls of the pit are almost eight feet high. They also are hard and smooth, offering little in the way of footholds. What's worse, the acrid smell in the pit is even worse than above ground.

As your eyes climb toward the sky, you notice a large, shadowy figure looming over you. The figure peers down at you from the edge of the pit. Then, still shadowy, it begins jumping up and down. A harsh, grunting sound emits from its mouth—its arms raised in victory.

The bear just got you.

This little tale is about objective-finding (O-F). Also known as "Mess-Finding," it is the first stage of the CPS process. It is in this stage that you start sensing your awareness of the challenges, concerns, and opportunities facing you. Then, you select one of these broad areas for further work.

In the story, the major character was faced with an ambiguous situation. He constantly evaluated his environment using all five senses. He also made a number of observations and formed some conclusions about what was going on and what he should do. Then, he made a choice and took action on it. Unfortunately, his choice did not work out so well (unless you have a "thing" about being trapped in pits).

With the CPS process, your choices should result in a more favorable outcome. By "playing" around with an ambiguous situation and gathering information, you should markedly increase your understanding of your objective. Of course, if you think you already understand your objective, then you probably won't need to spend much time in this stage. However, be sure you do understand your objective. Otherwise, you will risk throwing yourself off course for the remainder of the process.

OVERVIEW

As with the other CPS stages, objective-finding involves both divergent and convergent activities. Begin by diverging and gathering as much information as you can about the concerns, challenges, and opportunities facing you. Then, converge to evaluate the information you generated and select the most important objective area.

Isaksen and Treffinger (1985) suggest specific ways to structure the di-

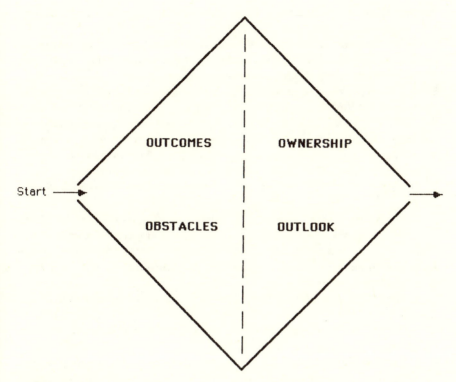

Figure 6–1
Objective-Finding

vergent and convergent aspects of objective-finding. Four of these suggestions are shown in Figure 6–1. The vertical, dotted line in this figure
represents the hypothetical dividing point between diverging and
converging.

Diverging involves assessing outcomes and obstacles. Outcomes are concerned with things you would like to achieve, while obstacles are what
might prevent you from achieving them. Converging involves assessments
of ownership and outlook. Ownership is your evaluation of the "stake"
you have in a particular concern, challenge, or opportunity. For example,
is the situation one over which you can exert some influence? Outlook, on
the other hand, deals with your general knowledge of the situation, such
as how important it is and how soon it must be dealt with.

DIVERGING: OUTCOMES AND OBSTACLES

Generating lists of outcomes and obstacles will help you structure the
divergent portion of objective-finding. These lists will provide you with a

specific focus for your efforts. In addition, listing outcomes and obstacles will make it easier to think of many potential objective areas. For some concerns, challenges, and opportunities, you will list more objectives using outcomes; for others, listing obstacles will be more productive. Thus, you should consider using both for most situations.

One way to facilitate making your lists is to use prompting statements such as: "Wouldn't it be nice if?" (WIBNI) for outcomes and "Wouldn't it be awful if?" (WIBAI) for obstacles. As with any divergent activity, you should defer all judgment when generating these statements. Let your thoughts flow and try for as many as you can. If you become blocked in your thinking, leave this task and do something else before returning.

To generate outcomes and obstacles, you might want to use the following steps:

1. List a variety of numbered WIBNI and WIBAI statements.

2. Select the statements that seem most interesting or relevant to you. That is, which statements best capture a major concern, challenge, or opportunity of yours? To do this, mark the statements in some way or rewrite their numbers.

3. Look over the statements you selected and see if they have anything in common.

4. If there are commonalities, select the one category that you would like to use as an objective area to work on.

5. Optional: Using this objective area as a stimulus, develop several tentative problem definitions. State these problems using the format: In what ways might I? (IWWMI). This step is optional, since it may be difficult at this point to develop specific problem statements for some situations. Use your best judgment.

To illustrate how outcomes might be formulated during divergence, some sample statements are presented next. Wouldn't it be nice if (step 1):

1. There were 30 hours in every day?
2. I only needed three hours of sleep per day?
3. I didn't have so many things I wanted to do?
4. I had a personal servant to do my bidding?
5. I could write two books at the same time?
6. I made a wish and something got done?
7. My thoughts were typed automatically?
8. My allergies disappeared completely?
9. My car never needed to be serviced?
10. I could learn through the process of osmosis?

In looking over these statements, I might decide that the most important ones for me are: 1, 3, 5, and 7 (step 2). Of these, 1 and 3 seem to have something in common in that both deal with time. The other two statements, 5 and 7, also seem to belong together (although they also are related to time), since they involve writing (step 3). I next choose time as the category I would like to work on (step 4). Finally, I use these statements in this category as stimulators and generate some tentative problem statements. For example, I might list such problems as: In what ways might I (step 5):

1. Organize my time better?
2. Better establish priorities?
3. Decrease the amount of work I have?
4. Delegate more work to others?
5. Have more control over my life?

To help you generate outcomes, there also are other formats you can try. For instance:

If nothing was impossible, I would. . . .
If I could do whatever I could visualize, I would. . . .
The one thing that needs to happen in my life is. . . .
If I was a magic genie, the first thing I would do is. . . .
Appoint me "director of everything" and I will. . . .
Grant me three wishes and I will. . . .
Give me a magic "twanger" and I will. . . .

Another way to stimulate your thinking about outcomes is to use a checklist of questions. Some examples follow, organized into who, what, where, when, why, and how categories:

1. Who usually helps you get something done?
2. Who is always willing to help you do something?
3. Who knows how to do something you always wanted to do?
4. Who are the best problem solvers you know? Who helps them solve problems?
5. Who can provide you with a major challenge?
6. What would you like to happen in your life?
7. What can you do to control your life more?
8. What usually happens when you try to do something new or different?
9. What mysteries would you like to solve today? Tomorrow? Next week? A month from now? A year from now?
10. What concerns you most about how you do something?
11. Where is the best place for you to get something done?
12. Where would you like to be right now?
13. Where can you get all the information you need about a situation?
14. Where do things happen that you like or identify with?
15. Where can you go to get help about most problems?
16. When do you most feel like accomplishing something?

17. When are you most comfortable? Happy? Satisfied?
18. When do you get the most done?
19. When do you know you have performed a task well?
20. When is it easiest for you to achieve a goal?
21. Why do you want to solve most of your problems?
22. Why do you enjoy a challenge?
23. Why can you have fun doing something that also is painful or difficult to do?
24. Why do you want to grow as a person?
25. Why do you like to create something new?
26. How can you solve your problems with less effort? With less anguish?
27. How can you be happy?
28. How can you achieve what you never have before?
29. How can you learn to be more efficient?
30. How can you improve yourself?

After answering these or other questions of your own, you should examine all of your responses. Then, use your responses to develop categories of objective areas.

The procedure for generating obstacle areas involves the same steps as described for outcomes. However, instead of beginning with WIBNI statements, you would start with WIBAI statements. For instance, wouldn't it be awful if (step 1):

1. I never could get any work done?
2. My computer broke down?
3. My car needed servicing every day?
4. I was unable to write?
5. I had no friends?
6. My children forgot who I was?
7. I had to pay twice as much income tax?
8. My life was shortened by five minutes every time I was impolite to someone?
9. I had plenty of time, but couldn't think of anything to do with it?
10. I was fired tomorrow for sitting around thinking: "WIBAI?" all of the time?

Next, I would look over these statements and select ones that seemed important to me or are of high interest to me. Thus, I might select questions 2, 4, 5, 6, and 10 (note that apparently I am willing to pay the price for being impolite) (step 2). After examining my choices, I then decide to form categories consisting of: writing concerns (questions 2 and 4), people concerns (questions 5 and 6), and a career concern (question 10) (step 3). I select career concerns as my major objective (step 4) and begin generating potential problem redefinitions (step 5). For instance, in what ways might I:

1. Achieve more job security?
2. Increase the variety of my job skills?
3. Decide what I want to do when I grow up?

4. Get my employer to beg me not to leave?

5. Get to know key people who could help me get another job?

Using a format similar to the one used to generate outcome statements, I also could use a variety of stimulators to help prompt obstacle statements. For example:

If nothing was possible, I never would be able to. . . .

If I could not visualize anything, I probably would lose an opportunity to. . . .

The one thing in my life that I hope never happens is. . . .

If my magic genie was inept, I would have to help him/her. . . .

Appoint me "director of nothing" and I will make sure that _____never happens.

If no one ever grants me three wishes, I never would be able to. . . .

If someone should neutralize my magic "twanger," it will stop me from. . . .

I also could look for additional statements by using obstacle-related question checklists. As with outcomes, these questions could be organized into who, what, where, when, why, and how categories. For example:

1. Who do you need to know to overcome most obstacles?
2. Who has the _____(fill in: money, power, influence, and so on) that often prevents you from doing something?
3. Who presents the greatest challenge to you?
4. Who do you fear most?
5. Who causes you the most problems?
6. What is bothering you right now? Yesterday? What do you think will be bothering you tomorrow?
7. What are the three worst things that could happen to you?
8. What would you like to influence more?
9. What always goes wrong when you try to do something new or different?
10. What are your major weaknesses?
11. Where would you least like to be right now?
12. Where did you go last for information that turned out wrong?
13. Where is the worst place for you to receive help for dealing with a problem?
14. Where are the biggest obstacles in your life?
15. Where else are there obstacles in your life?
16. When do you feel most frustrated?
17. When are you least successful at solving problems?
18. When do you least feel like exploring concerns, challenges, and opportunities?
19. When do you have the most trouble achieving a goal?
20. When do you feel as if you are losing ground when working toward a goal?
21. Why did you miss your last big opportunity?
22. Why do you stop working on some of your problems?
23. Why do you dread facing some situations?

24. Why do some problems seem incapable of being solved?
25. Why do you sometimes have trouble recognizing problem situations you should deal with?
26. How can you recognize obstacles more easily?
27. How can you overcome obstacles more efficiently?
28. How can you learn more about yourself?
29. How do other people learn about their obstacles in life?
30. How can you gain more resources to deal with your obstacles?

After examining these questions or others of your own, write down any new objective areas you might think of. Then, add these areas to your master list.

CONVERGING: OWNERSHIP AND OUTLOOK

At this point in the CPS process, you should be ready to converge and choose an objective area. However, at no time should you feel "locked in." If you should change your mind about what is a priority to you, feel free to select another. You even may want to return to diverging and generate more information. Whatever you do, choose an area you feel comfortable with.

The ownership phase of converging is designed to help you select an area of high personal importance to you—an area in which you feel you must produce a solution. The outlook phase during convergence allows you to test your awareness of the objective area you have chosen and consider criteria for selecting a final area.

Ownership. You "own" a problem when you have some influence over and are motivated to deal with it. For instance, if you are a manager you might see yourself in sole possession of a situation involving a decrease in client orders. You can influence the situation by seeking information and altering key variables. You also will need the motivation to deal with it.

On the other hand, there also are situations in which you can share ownership with others. Depending upon the variables of influence and motivation, others also may have a stake in your objective area. For instance, your subordinates might want to help increase the number of client orders if they work under a profit-sharing agreement or are otherwise motivated.

If an objective area is one in which you do not have exclusive ownership, you may want to reconsider dealing with it. Otherwise, working with someone else may be difficult due to differences in perceived influence and motivation. In such situations, you might be able to select a portion of an area over which you have complete ownership and focus upon it. Or, if there is sufficient time, you might try using group problem solving if the group's perceptions of influence and motivation are not too different.

To begin the convergent portion of objective-finding, you should use the criteria of influence and motivation to select problem statements for further consideration. If a problem statement from the divergent phase does not satisfy the criteria of influence and motiviation, you might eliminate it. However, I prefer to use a more cautious approach. I usually set aside such statements for future consideration. I am especially likely to do this when a statement satisfies one of the criteria. You, of course, will have to use your own judgment.

Outlook. Assessing outlook criteria is the final step in selecting an objective area to work on. Isaksen and Treffinger (1985) suggest using the criteria of: familiarity, critical nature, immediacy, and stability.

Familiarity is important, since the more you know about your area, the easier it will be to deal with. If you are not knowledgeable about an area, you will have to devote some time to learning about it. As a result, you might want to reject areas involving high investments of time or effort.

Critical nature is an important criterion for obvious reasons. You probably devote most of your problem solving efforts to important areas. If you view a problem as relatively trivial and unlikely to result in serious consequences, you might reject it (or at least set it aside for future consideration).

Immediacy needs to be considered when evaluating problems, since timing often is of extreme importance. You can put off some problems for months or even years. Other problems, in contrast, require immediate or short-range attention.

Stability, the fourth criterion, concerns the likelihood that a situation will change over time. Some situations may be more likely than others to increase in severity over time. When it is possible for you to make an accurate assessment, you should assign a high priority to situations that may get worse unless something is done (e.g., many health problems).

If you can't select an objective area to work on after completing the convergent phase, reassess how you used the CPS model. You might want to start over again and generate additional objective areas. Or, you might decide that you already have a good idea of what your problem is. In this case, you could jump ahead to one of the other CPS stages, depending upon how well you understand your problem.

GUIDELINES FOR TRAINERS

There are several points about the objective-finding stage that you should emphasize:

1. Although all the CPS stages are important, this stage is especially important. It is vital that users get off to a good start. Otherwise, they may encounter numerous unnecessary complications later on. In particular, if

users don't identify the objective area they most need to work on, subsequent efforts may lack focus and result in much frustration.

I recently participated in a group that was attempting to identify project areas of common interest. The facilitator, who was moderately experienced in using CPS, decided to begin with the problem-finding stage. The result was considerable frustration. There was much uncertainty about how to word the problems and disagreement over the content areas. This should have been a clue that either objective-finding or fact-finding was skipped over prematurely.

2. However, if there already is a clearly defined objective area, very little (if any) attention should be devoted to this stage. Otherwise, the "wrong" area may be selected (i.e., wrong in the sense of not being a priority area for an individual or group). In groups, this caution has special significance, since there frequently will not be total agreement as to the most vital objective area.

3. Objective areas consist primarily of concerns, challenges, and opportunities (although other topics could be added, such as experiences, feelings, etc.). Avoid using the word "problem" when discussing objective areas. Instead, reserve this word for statements generated as a result of evaluating objective areas.

Although this distinction may appear subtle, it is relatively important. The word "problem" often has unpleasant connotations associated with it. For some people, this word may evoke emotions or images of an almost insurmountable obstacle. Consequently, it is better to use a more neutral and positive term. The words "concern," "challenge," and "opportunity" also have an almost empowering quality about them that can help motivate people.

4. Make a "big deal" about the dividing line between divergence and convergence. As shown in figure 6–1, these two phases should be separated during objective-finding. Objectives must be generated before they are evaluated.

5. During divergence, emphasize the importance of really "stretching" when generating objective areas. Tell the group to withhold all evaluation and list as many areas as possible.

6. When discussing converging and diverging, place special emphasis upon the convergent phase. Although examining outcomes and obstacles helps generate objective area statements, many people don't need structured aids. During convergence, however, a more structured approach can help narrow down the data generated.

The most important point to make about convergence is the need to be realistic. There must be clear-cut ownership and a favorable outlook in regard to chosen objective areas. Encourage the class to pay special attention to these considerations. Failure to do so now could lead to major difficulties later on.

7. You might recall that listing problem redefinitions was optional during divergence and convergence (step 5). It may be premature to focus upon specific problem statements at this time. Too narrow a perspective might restrict users unduly. Instead, encourage class members to use their best judgment and decide if they feel comfortable developing definitions. If they are very uncertain about their objective area during divergence, they probably should put off listing any problem definitions. However, they may feel more comfortable at the end of divergence or even convergence. The point is: Be flexible and don't insist that definitions be developed only so the model can be "properly" followed.

8. The stimulator questions for generating objective area statements usually help most people (e.g., grant me three wishes and I will . . .). However, don't limit the class to these questions alone. Encourage them to develop and experiment with their own questions when dealing with outcomes and obstacles.

In addition to these pointers and other information in this chapter, there are several methods to help group members sharpen their skills of divergence. The ones discussed next are borrowed from creativity consultants Steve Grossman (1985) and Sidney Parnes (1985b).

Grossman suggests developing a symbol of a desired future state and describing its characteristics. Then, use these characteristics to generate possible objective areas.

For example, a newspaper publisher might describe a desired future state using an umbrella as a symbol. The umbrella might be described as providing only partial coverage of the whole body, providing full coverage of the head, and having bent ribs, a carved handle, and holes in the fabric. These descriptors then could generate such objective areas as: increase circulation (partial coverage), improve liability insurance (full coverage of the head), reinforce the structure of the plant walls (bent ribs), carve out a new niche of readers (carved handle), and plug all security leaks (holes in the fabric).

Parnes suggests a variety of relatively simple procedures for generating potential objective areas. Among his many suggestions are: visualization, telegrams and headlines, and crayon drawings. Some people may find all three procedures useful, while others may prefer only one. Experimenting and practicing is the only way to learn which will work best. Before you use any of these methods, try to become as relaxed as possible.

One way to use visualization (based upon Parnes' ideas and some of my own) is to first select some general situation you are concerned about. Try to visualize several different scenes that capture the "essence" of the situation. Select one of these scenes and pretend you are watching it on a TV screen. Write down whatever reactions you have while watching. Select another scene and do the same. Finally, look over everything you have written and list any objective areas that are suggested.

Using telegrams and headlines to generate objective areas is very basic and straightforward. Although this method works well during the early portion of divergence, it probably is most useful during the latter portion.

To use this method, write a one sentence description of some concern, challenge, or opportunity. When you write down your description, pretend you are doing it for a very expensive telegram or newspaper headline (this restriction should force you to be quite economical in your description). For instance, you might write down something like: WRITER NEEDS MORE TIME TO WRITE or SEND HELP. MANAGER BESIEGED BY UNHAPPY CUSTOMERS. This method works especially well in groups where the telegrams or headlines can be shared and discussed. Moreover, they can help stimulate others to think of objective areas.

Crayon drawings are another simple way to list objective area statements. Give each person a small box of crayons and ask them to draw a picture that represents a major concern, challenge, or opportunity in their life. Instruct them to elaborate as much as possible and to use as many colors as they want. Also, instruct them to avoid being too literal and, instead, include some abstract symbols.

When all the drawings are completed, have the participants examine their drawings and use them as stimuli for possible objective areas. Make sure they spend some time carefully analyzing all symbols represented and any implications for objective areas. For instance, a heavy line separating two distinct sections on a paper might suggest some major obstacle. This obstacle should be identified and written down as a potential objective area.

In case you haven't thought of it, all of these suggestions also will apply to the divergent portions of other stages in the model. A few modifications may be required, but otherwise most of the suggestions should be workable for most divergent activities.

SUMMARY

Objective-finding, the first stage of the CPS process, is designed to help explore and select a primary concern, challenge, or opportunity to work on. Like the other CPS stages, objective-finding uses divergent and convergent activities. During divergence, you should gather as much information as you can about a situation that concerns you and generate many possible objective areas. During convergence, you should try to narrow down these objective areas and select one with the highest priority to you.

Divergence can be aided by examining outcomes and obstacles. Outcomes can be generated using a question preface such as: "Wouldn't it be nice if (WIBNI)?"; obstacles can be generated in a like manner using a question such as: "Wouldn't it be awful if (WIBAI)?" Other questions and statements also can help generate objective areas.

Convergence can be aided by examining the variables of ownership and outlook. Ownership is used to determine if the objective area is one you can influence and if you are motivated to deal with it. Outlook is used to assess how familiar you are with a chosen objective area (familiarity), how important the area is to you (critical nature), how soon it needs to be dealt with (immediacy), and how likely it is to change over time (stability). Obviously, you should try to deal with objectives you "own" and ones that have a favorable outlook.

When trainers present material on objective-finding, there are several points they should emphasize:

1. As the first stage of the CPS process, special care should be taken to select the "right" objective area. Future success in using the model will be determined, in part, by this choice.

2. Users should feel free to leave objective-finding at any time if they are certain of their objective.

3. Avoid use of the word "problem" until your primary objective area has been selected. Discourage class members from using this word during the early stages of divergence in objective-finding.

4. Strongly emphasize the importance of separating the divergent and convergent portions of objective-finding.

5. Make sure that users really "stretch" for objectives when diverging and that all evaluation is deferred until converging.

6. Note that converging is especially important, since a realistic objective statement must be chosen to ensure success during CPS.

7. Generally speaking, participants should avoid forming specific problem definitions during divergence or convergence. However, this is not an inviolable rule. Individual judgment should be used in all cases.

8. Encourage participants to develop their own questions and statements to use as stimulation for generating objectives.

In addition to the methods described, there are other techniques that can stimulate objective areas. For example: select a symbol representing a desired future state and use elaborations of it as stimulation, or use visualization, telegrams and headlines, or abstract crayon drawings.

7
Fact-Finding

The woman rambled on and on and on. She discussed everything except what she had just been asked. Joe turned to his partner and slowly rolled his eyes upward. They had been through this hundreds of times before. Ask a simple question and you get someone's life story.

Joe knew how to fix such situations. He had a ready response that never failed. He looked directly into the woman's eyes and said, "Just the facts, ma'am. Just the facts."

If you happen to remember the old television show, Dragnet, you probably remember Sergeant Joe Friday's statement. It seems that Sergeant Friday was somewhat impatient. When questioning someone about a crime, he wanted only relevant information. He had little use for the irrelevant.

The fact-finding stage of CPS most likely would be Sergeant Friday's favorite stage. During this stage, your primary task is to gather as much data as you can about your objective area. However, these data should be limited to "just the facts." You want to increase your understanding of your objective so later on you can consider different problem perspectives (problem-finding) and begin generating potential solutions (idea-finding).

When you first deal with any situation, there is a certain amount of data that will be relevant. Some data may pertain directly to your objective, some may be only slightly relevant, and other data may appear to be totally irrelevant. During fact-finding, your task is to separate the relevant from the irrelevant and begin establishing some priority areas.

Of course, you may be confident that you already understand your problem and know everything you can or need to know about it. If so, skip this stage and move on to problem-finding. However, before you make such a decision, devote some effort to gathering a few facts just to be certain.

Otherwise, you risk dealing with the "wrong" problem during the rest of the CPS process.

ADVANTAGES OF FACT-FINDING

In one respect, fact-finding serves as an extension of objective-finding. During fact-finding, you continue to refine your understanding of a particular concern, challenge, or opportunity. Unlike objective-finding, however, you now have identified the general area in which you want to focus your efforts. The outcome of fact-finding should be a specific problem area that you can explore in more depth during problem-finding.

Like objective-finding and problem-finding, fact-finding helps avoid premature closure of a problem. It allows you to remain problem oriented instead of becoming solution oriented. As a result, you are more likely to end up working upon the "real" problem.

Another advantage is that fact-finding may help uncover an unanticipated or overlooked aspect of an objective area. You might think you have considered everything about a situation when you really haven't. Or, you might discover something that you had not considered previously. In either case, such facts eventually could prove crucial for resolving a problem situation. Taking the time to search for such facts can make the difference between success and failure.

Fact-finding also helps uncover new ways of viewing your objective area. Additional data sometimes can provide the new perspective vital to increased understanding and problem resolution.

Finally, fact-finding helps determine your priority areas. If you haven't already identified this area during objective-finding, now is the time to do so. Fact-finding will allow you to pinpoint this area so you can start considering alternative problem perspectives.

OVERVIEW

The divergent phase of fact-finding involves generating (without evaluation) as much data as you can about your general objective area. During the convergent phase, you try to identify priority areas. The outcome of this stage should be at least one written statement of a problem.

As shown in Figure 7–1, various techniques can aid divergent and convergent fact-finding activities. For instance, during divergence, you could begin by considering your observations, feelings, knowledge, and thoughts. To draw out relevant information about your objective area, use the "five W's and H" method (who, what, where when, why, how). A general checklist of questions also can be used to help identify data. During convergence, you should focus upon "hits," "relates," "critical concerns," and

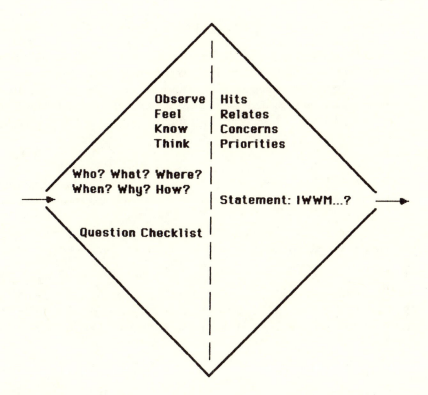

Figure 7–1
Fact-Finding

"priorities." Finally, you should develop a tentative problem definition using the words: In what ways might (IWWM)?

DIVERGING

The divergent phase of fact-finding is where you should learn everything you can about your objective area. You might think you understand it, but a little digging around often can change your mind. As you begin to uncover new information and put together the pieces, entirely new perspectives might emerge.

Most of us probably don't diverge enough during fact-finding. According to Cotton (1984), we often stop searching for data for a number of reasons. For example, we might settle for the first bit of data we uncover. If it appears plausible or highly relevant, it is easier to stop than continue looking. We also tend to define problems in terms of people rather than situations. That is, it is simpler to blame someone than to identify a situational factor that might be involved. Finally, we sometimes overlook "nonevents" or "nonoccurrences." Facts that are not immediately apparent often prove to be the most useful. Thus, if a house dog that normally barks suddenly becomes silent, the lack of barking might indicate something significant.

Perhaps the most important guideline to remember during divergence is to defer all judgment. Generate all the data you can about your objective area during divergence. Save all your evaluative comments for convergence. If you have the time and the problem is important to you, try to learn as much as you can about the problem.

One way to begin diverging is to examine your observations, feelings, knowledge, and thoughts about your objective area. You need to absorb as much as you can to increase your understanding. Don't limit yourself to what you believe you know. Instead, systematically search for as much data as possible.

Observations are anything you hear, see, taste, touch, or smell. Thus, you should consider whatever your senses tell you. Feelings refer to your emotional reactions—how you respond affectively to a situation. Knowledge pertains to the specific facts you have. Although you should avoid confusing facts and opinions, don't totally exclude opinions. Many opinions often will fall into one of the other categories. Finally, thoughts refer to your subjective impressions. These impressions may be no more than mere hunches.

When generating fact-finding data, don't be limited by what you personally have experienced. Instead, stretch and try to imagine what else the situation might look like, feel like, and so forth. The validity of your data during this phase is not important. Record everything you can and then evaluate it during the convergent phase.

After recording your general observations, knowledge, feelings, and thoughts, try a slightly more systematic way of gathering data. One method that often works well is the "five W's and H" method. To use this method, pose questions about your objective area, beginning each question with either a who, what, where, when, why, or how. Then, look over all of your responses and use them as stimuli for developing new perspectives.

Suppose, for example, that your objective area involves finding ways to have more time available for personal affairs. Although greatly simplified, a five W's and H procedure might be set up as follows:

Question	*Response*
Who would like more time?	I would; people who are disorganized.
What decreases time available?	Lack of attention; failure to establish priorities.
Where do people have enough time?	Where a framework or system is used to guide how jobs get done.

When is time least available?	During very busy periods; when I want it most.
Why do I need more time?	To do a better job; to accomplish more.
How could I acquire more time?	Seek the advice of others; reorganize tasks; rearrange priorities.

After generating these and many other questions and answers, I then would use the responses to suggest different viewpoints. Thus, instead of concentrating upon organizing time, I eventually might decide to redirect my efforts to better organize my tasks or revise my priorities.

A third way to diverge for data is to use a general checklist of questions. As you did with the five W's and H method, answer each question and use it as a stimulus for generating new problem perspectives. Some examples of such questions follow:

1. What do you know about the situation?
2. Who else could help you deal with this situation? Why?
3. What would be better if you resolved this situation? What would be worse?
4. Are some aspects of the objective area more important than others? If so, which ones and why are they more important?
5. How would someone you respect deal with this situation?
6. What is the major obstacle facing you in dealing with this situation?
7. What will things be like if you resolve this situation?
8. What assumptions do you still need to test about this situation?
9. What is the most prominent feature of this situation? The least prominent feature?
10. How does this situation relate to others you have dealt with? What is similar? What is dissimilar?
11. What parts of the situation are related?
12. When is the situation likely to get worse? Get better?
13. What's good about this situation? What do you like least about it? Like best?
14. When you first encountered this situation, what was your reaction?
15. What have you done to deal with the situation so far? Have you been successful? Why or why not?

To illustrate some of the basic principles underlying fact-finding, a simple awareness exercise sometimes can help. A drawing of my computer is shown in Figure 7–2. Using this drawing, write down all the facts you know about the computer. Don't limit yourself only to what you are certain about; also consider what might exist as well as what you might infer. Even without much knowledge of computers, you should be able to generate a fairly long list.

Examples of some data I extracted from the drawing are:

1. The computer is an Apple Macintosh.
2. The keyboard and other peripherals are missing.

Figure 7–2
Computer Exercise

3. There is a screen and slot for a disk on the front.
4. Air vents are on the side and top.
5. Some sort of mark or insignia is on the lower left front.
6. The front bottom portion has a "notch" in it.
7. This "notch" can accommodate the keyboard.
8. There is a built-in handhold on the top for carrying.
9. Due to the single disk drive, disks need to be swapped to copy a document from one disk to another (or a second disk drive needs to be added).
10. It is relatively light in weight.
11. It is portable.
12. It can be connected to a printer.
13. It requires software to be used.
14. Electricity is needed to run it.
15. An on/off switch turns it on and off.
16. The brightness of the screen can be adjusted.
17. Editing is easy using word-processing programs.
18. Pictures easily can be drawn and edited using graphics programs.
19. A magnetic field near the computer could damage any data contained on disks.
20. A large amount of dust or other foreign substances could damage the computer if it affected vital parts.
21. Software can be expensive to purchase.
22. The computer uses a "mouse" to perform various operations.
23. In the front lower right portion of the computer, there is an opening for connecting the keyboard.
24. Most software programs run by this computer use pulldown "menus."
25. Some homeowners' insurance policies cover the computer at home, but not at an office.
26. Many people are afraid to even try using computers.
27. I would shrivel and die if I could not use my computer.
28. You don't need programming knowledge to use a computer.
29. Many computer programs are not compatible with programs designed for other types of computers.
30. A newspaper article recently described a forthcoming meeting of computer manufacturers to discuss standardizing computers for greater compatibility.

In generating my list, I tried to restrict my statements to those familiar to most people. You probably thought of many other statements. However, you shouldn't compare my list with yours, since individual problem solving is a personal matter. That is, we all have or are searching for problem ownership.

One thing you should have noticed during this exercise is that it probably wasn't as difficult as you first imagined. You initially may have thought of only a few facts and wondered how you ever could come up with more. However, by playing around with some facts and using previous facts for stimulation, diverging for data can be relatively easy. Knowing when to stop often is more difficult.

When to stop diverging. If you are successful at diverging during fact-finding, you should reach a point where you must decide how much is enough. One major guideline to use when making this decision is: Quit diverging once several areas of importance keep appearing. Often, these areas will be related in some way and cluster around some central theme (or themes) important to you.

When using the five W's and H method, you also might consider stopping divergence when your responses to different questions are essentially the same. If your responses begin to repeat, you may be looking at an area of significance to you. However, don't quit at this point unless you have spent some time generating data. Otherwise, your fact-finding search may be too limited.

CONVERGING

Now that you have generated a mass of data about your objective area, you need to do something with it. Specifically you need to examine it and use only information that will be most useful. Once you have isolated data that are relevant to you, you will be ready to refine your problem more.

Converging can be difficult if you have generated a lot of data. In fact, you might not even know where to begin. However, there are techniques that can help.

These techniques provide a systematic way for narrowing down the data you have collected and "squeezing" out the essence. It is important that your approach be systematic. Otherwise, you might overlook some important data. Thus, if you have the time, spend some effort reviewing your data.

The basic elements involved in converging are known as "hits," "relates," "critical concerns," and "priorities" (Treffinger, Isaksen & Firestein, 1983). Each one is designed to assist you in further narrowing down your data and extracting the most useful elements.

To begin converging, review all the data you have collected and note what appears to be important in relation to your objective area. These "hits" should be items you consider interesting or particularly relevant to your objective. Highlight your hits using some sort of mark or notation (e.g., write an "H" beside each hit or use a highlighting pen).

Next, look over your hits and identify any commonalities that might exist. Such collections of hits are known as "relates." Depending upon the quantity and quality of your data, you may have only a few or very many relates.

Evaluating the relates is the third step of the convergent process. Examine all the relates and decide which groups of data represent the "critical concerns." That is, which clusters of hits best capture the essence of your general problem?

Finally, the last step in the process involves assigning priorities to the critical concerns you have identified. In most situations, some critical concerns will appear to be more important than others. This difference can be due to a number of factors. For instance, some things may need to be done before others, the cost of deferring some things may justify an earlier priority, and so forth.

The basic concepts of hits, relates, critical concerns, and priorities can be illustrated more vividly using a visual illustration. One way of representing these concepts is shown in figure 7–3. The large patterned area represents the total field of data available to you. Within this field, you identify bits of data (the small circles with a "D"). Next, you identify data hits ("DH"). The hits that appear related can be clustered as shown by the heavy dark circles. After examining these clusters, you identify two of them as critical concerns ("CC" in the figure). Of these two, the one indicated by "P" is selected as a priority area for you to work on.

To give you a more concrete example, assume that I work in the computer field (not likely). I already have done objective-finding and generated the data on the computer example discussed previously. The 30 statements from this example are individual bits of data about the picture of the computer (the "D's").

First, I select item numbers 2, 3, 4, 9, 10, 14, 17, 18, 19, 20, 29, and 30 as my data hits (DH). Next, I look for relates. In looking over the data hits, I group them into three areas: components (items 2, 3, and 4), advantages (items 10, 17, 18, and 30), and disadvantages (items 9, 14, 19, 20, 29, and 30). Third, I select one or more critical concerns. In this case, I might choose the components and disadvantages categories. Finally, I choose the disadvantages as my priority area.

At this point, I could use this category to generate a tentative problem definition. In looking over the items in this category, however, I note that the disadvantages also might be clustered. For example, I could group items 9 and 14 into a category involving ease of use of the computer; items 19 and 20 into a category involving potential damage to the computer; and

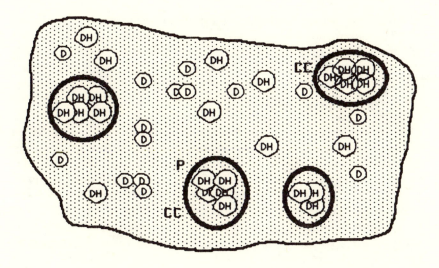

D = DATA   CC = CRITICAL CONCERNS

DH = DATA HITS   P = PRIORITY AREAS

Figure 7–3
Illustration of the Convergent Process

items 29 and 30 into a category involving computer compatibility. Of these three areas, I might select computer compatibility as my first priority, potential damage as my second area, and ease of use as my third.

This illustration of the convergent process is based upon my perceptions. Someone else dealing with the same situation might produce different outcomes. For instance, someone else might decide that the disadvantage category is satisfactory and doesn't need to be broken down further.

At this point, you should have a fairly clear idea as to the area you want to investigate further. If so, your final fact-finding activity is to write down a tentative problem statement for your priority area. (If you have chosen more than one priority area, write a separate statement for each.)

To write this statement, look over the priority area and state the primary concern, challenge, or opportunity involved. Use the question format: In what ways might (IWWM)? Thus, with the area of computer compatibility, I might develop such statements as: IWWM our company contribute toward compatibility of computer hardware? IWWM we help develop standards of computer software compatibility? IWWM we encourage the computer industry to base its software upon the same operating system?

If you still are uncertain about your primary concern, challenge, or opportunity, you might have trouble generating problem statements. If so, write down what you consider to be the important elements of your priority area. These elements then will form the basis for problem statement development during problem-finding.

GUIDELINES FOR TRAINERS

Fact-finding obviously is an important stage in the CPS model. When discussing this stage with a class, emphasize its importance in increasing understanding of the objective area. Premature closure could be disastrous at this point. Therefore, note that fact-finding provides an opportunity to explore further a situation and perhaps uncover new information not previously considered. Failure to take the time to gather relevant data could lead to further confusion and ambiguity about a situation.

After this discussion, you might provide a brief overview of fact-finding. Stress that there are no absolutes—that the techniques described in this chapter are suggested and not required. Each person will have to decide what will work best in any given situation. For instance, it won't always be necessary to use the five W's and H method or a checklist of stimulator questions. Such techniques are designed only to help and not to hinder the process.

To illustrate the basic principles underlying divergence and convergence, have your class practice with a variety of exercises. During the diverging exercises, emphasize the need to really "stretch" when generating data. Encourage the class to push themselves to think of as many bits of data as they can.

To introduce divergence, discuss the exercise involving the computer. Then, have the class do another exercise in small groups using another object. After doing this, ask what was easy and what was difficult about the exercise. Also, ask for any suggestions on how individual members were able to "stretch" their thinking. For instance, many people divide an object into discrete parts and functions and then diverge using these parts.

Another useful divergence exercise is to select a short article from a newspaper, magazine, or even a company publication. Have class members individually read it. Then, divide them into small groups and ask them to generate as much data as they can about the article. (The data should be generated without regard to their importance.)

If you practice with the stimulator questions, encourage your class to generate their own lists. This could be done individually, within small groups, or as a whole class. Ideally, their questions should focus upon work-related issues and topics. Such a list might be more useful than a more general one.

When talking about how to end divergence, have the class members suggest their own criteria for termination. One way to begin would be to take a sample list of data and ask if more data are needed. Then, discuss the variety and types of criteria involved.

Once your class has practiced diverging, use the data generated to practice converging. When describing use of hits, relates, critical concerns, and priorities, emphasize the need to be flexible. Not all situations will dictate rigid use of these mechanisms. For example, it may be possible to zero in on priorities of some data sets, while others will require substantially more shifting and sorting to identify important areas.

You also should note the need to be flexible when categorizing data. As demonstrated in the example, even final priority areas may need to be analyzed further and broken down into more refined priorities. Or, it may be necessary to combine priority areas. The process is subjective and based upon individual perceptions. Therefore, avoid teaching the "right" way to converge on the data.

SUMMARY

Fact-finding is designed to increase understanding of an objective area. To do this, gather as much relevant data as possible about your general problem situation. Then, select the most important data and develop a tentative problem definition.

There are several advantages to the fact-finding stage. Fact-finding helps avoid premature problem closure, increases the odds of uncovering unanticipated or overlooked data, provides new perspectives on your objective area, and assists in determining your priority area.

Diverging during fact-finding can be aided by certain techniques. For instance, you might begin by considering your observations, feelings, knowledge, and thoughts about the objective area. Another method involves developing a list of "five W's and H" questions (who, what, where, when, why, how) about your objective area. You can use your responses to these questions for developing new perspectives. Another approach involves using a ready-made list of general stimulation questions. The most important consideration when diverging is to defer all evaluation until the convergent phase.

In general, you should stop diverging whenever several areas important to you keep appearing. If you are using the five W's and H technique, you probably should stop diverging if your responses begin to repeat.

Converging during fact-finding involves looking for hits, relates, critical concerns, and priorities. Hits are data you consider to be important; relates are clusters of hits with something in common; critical concerns are the relates you consider to be most important; and priorities are your most important critical concerns. The final convergent activity involves using the priority area or areas you have identified to suggest a tentative problem statement.

Due to its importance to the CPS process, trainers should provide their classes with plenty of fact-finding practice. This can be done using a variety of exercises and data relevant to class members. Trainers should emphasize and model a flexible approach and avoid being tied rigidly to one particular technique.

8
Problem-Finding

The problem-finding stage of CPS is similar to what a detective might go through when trying to solve a murder mystery. However, contrary to what a Sherlock Holmes character might suggest, there is more than just logic involved. Both analytical and creative skills are required.

The detective must begin by clarifying objectives and selecting the most promising challenge represented by the murder (objective-finding). Next, he must gather all relevant facts that might help unravel key elements involved (fact-finding). The facts selected during this process should uncover the most promising approach to pursue. Then, the detective needs to consider a variety of perspectives (problem-finding). After choosing one of these perspectives, he should be ready to generate possible courses of action that will lead to solution of the crime.

Viewed this way, objective-finding and fact-finding pave the way for problem-finding. The first two stages funnel your energy and effort toward development of a problem statement you can use to generate potential solutions. How you state your problem at the end of the problem-finding stage will determine, in part, how successful you will be at generating ideas and, eventually, solving your problem. This is why problem-finding is such an important stage.

For many of us, "finding" a problem can be a difficult task. Throughout our lives, we are given problems to solve. In school, our teachers gave us problems in different subjects and instructed us to come up with the "correct" solution. In the world of work, things are not much different. However, many work-related problem situations have no correct solutions. In many instances, we may be forced to find a problem and then come up with a variety of potential solutions.

The primary purpose of problem-finding is to help you develop a statement of the "real" problem. A "real" problem, of course, is one that is most important to you. It is the problem statement that most productively focuses your efforts toward generating potential solutions. After selecting this statement, your ideas should flow easily. If they don't, you may have selected an inappropriate statement or only a part of the situation you need to resolve. When this occurs, you should consider another problem perspective.

IMPORTANCE OF PROBLEM-FINDING

Scientists have long recognized the importance of finding the "correct" problem. For example, as noted in Chapter 3, Einstein believed that finding a problem is more important than finding a solution; the latter requires primarily routine skills, while problem finding relies upon imagination (Einstein & Infeld, 1938).

In a similar vein, the educator/philosopher John Dewey noted that "discovering a problem is the first step in knowing" (Dewey, 1938). And Wertheimer (1959) observed that: "Often in great discoveries the most important thing is that a certain question is found. Envisaging, putting the productive question is often more important, often a greater achievement than solution of a set question" (p. 123).

The car story previously described in Chapter 2 perhaps best illustrates the importance of problem-finding. If you recall, the way the occupants of the two cars with flat tires defined their problem determined their eventual success. The occupants of the first car defined their problem as: "In what ways might we get a jack?" The second car's occupants chose the definition: "In what ways might we raise our car?"

By using a relatively broad definition, the second group was able to choose from a wider number of options. In marked contrast, the occupants of the first group were severely limited in their options. Their narrow definition restricted their options to borrowing a jack from the service station.

Like many of us, you probably have limited your options often by defining a problem too narrowly. Devoting a little effort to problem-finding, however, can open up new ways of viewing your situation.

OVERVIEW

The major elements involved in problem-finding are shown in Figure 8–1. The divergent phase begins with a review of the data generated during fact-finding. This is followed by a listing of ownership and action elements that might contribute to potential problem redefinitions. Next, you might use techniques such as key words or the "why method" to explore the boundaries of your problem situation. Finally, you should generate as many

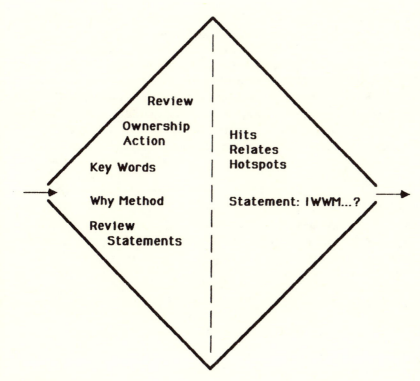

Figure 8–1
Problem-Finding

possible redefinitions as you can. The convergent phase is similar to the convergent phases of other stages. The first set of activities involves identification of hits, relates, and hotspots as they pertain to your redefinitions. The final activity is to select one final statement to use as a springboard for idea-finding.

PROBLEM REDEFINITIONS

Before examining divergence, the general nature of problem statements needs to be examined. Problem-finding works best when appropriate statements are used. Just any old statement won't do.

When you begin problem-finding, you already may have developed an explicit statement of your problem. If not, you probably have a tentative idea as to what you think your problem is. During problem-finding, you will have the opportunity to "stretch" this perception and redefine your statement in many ways.

Problem statements appropriate for CPS have three major elements: an "invitational stem," an ownership component, and an action component (Isaksen & Treffinger, 1985). Although such terms might lead you to expect an English lesson next, be assured that I have no such intention. However, you need to understand the best format for redefinitions to increase the odds of producing high-quality solutions.

The invitational stem for all statements is: "In what ways might (IWWM)?" Beginning a statement with this phrase allows for and encourages a divergent response. In contrast, beginning a statement with the word "how," for example, is more likely to direct you to one possible response. Thus, the invitational stem, IWWM?, helps avoid premature problem closure.

A problem statement that fails to specify who will do what is virtually useless. If nobody understands who owns a problem, nobody is likely to do anything about it. Thus, a "good" problem statement must have some indication of who owns it.

In a similar manner, a good problem statement also must have some indication of an action verb (or verb phrase) specified. It isn't enough just to identify the "who." You also need to specify what will be done. In addition, the action component should spell out the goal or objective area.

To illustrate these major components, consider the following problem statements:

1. IWWM I reduce stress on my job?
2. IWWM students pay less tuition?
3. IWWM I receive a raise?

The invitational stem, ownership, and action and goal components are pretty evident for these statements. In the first statement, ownership is "I," the action verb is "reduce," and the goal is "stress on the job." For statement two, "students" is the ownership element, "pay" is the verb, and "less tuition" is the goal. The third statement's ownership element is "I," "receive" is the action, and "raise" is the goal element.

Writing good problem statements requires practice. Most novices commit a variety of errors that can be avoided easily by following a few basic guidelines. When writing problem statements, remember the following rules of thumb:

1. Avoid including problem criteria in your statements.
2. Generate as many statements as you can.
3. Keep your statements as brief as possible; be concise.
4. Don't be afraid to list "silly" statements.
5. Always include ownership and action components.
6. Include only one problem area at a time in each statement.

7. If you are dissatisfied with your statements, use stimulator techniques (to be discussed in this chapter) or recycle to objective-finding or fact-finding.

Of these guidelines, three are probably most typical of the novice statement writer. The first involves a tendency to make statements too wordy. This often is the result of two other errors: including criteria and including more than one problem area.

The reason for keeping statements concise should be evident. A concise statement is easier to understand and use for generating ideas. Avoiding criteria in statements is especially important since doing so can inhibit your creativity. If you restrict yourself before generating ideas, your ideas are likely to be limited in scope. As a result, you may not uncover ideas with the highest potential. You can apply criteria later, during the convergent phase of idea-finding.

The importance of restricting a statement to one problem area also should be evident. Generating ideas requires a focus upon one specific area. If you have to switch back and forth between two or more areas, it will be more difficult to concentrate and think of ideas. For instance, you might modify the statement about receiving a raise to read: "IWWM I receive a raise and get along better with my co-workers?" In this case, there clearly are two separate problems (unless a salary difference affects the way you view your co-workers).

As far as the other guidelines are concerned, their importance also should be self-evident: generating as many definitions as you can will help increase the odds of developing high-quality statements (i.e., ones with the potential to suggest the "essence" of your problem situation); not being afraid to list "silly" statements will help your creative juices stimulate higher quality statements; including the appropriate components obviously will help ensure a better statement; and using stimulators to prompt statements or recycling to previous stages will help generate a variety of statements.

DIVERGING

There are a number of techniques you can use to help stimulate problem statements. How many you use is up to you, given your personal preferences, how important you consider your objective area to be, and the amount of time available. If you were to use all of the divergent techniques described in this chapter, you might proceed as follows:

1. Review all of the data you generated during fact-finding. Pay particular attention to the critical concerns and priorities you identified. Then, use this information as stimulation for generating problem statements.

2. Based upon what you know about your general problem, develop separate lists of every possible ownership and action element. Be sure to withhold all evaluation when doing this. Otherwise, you might overlook

an aspect you failed to consider previously. Examine different combinations from each list and see what problem statements are suggested.

3. Develop a list of alternate, "key" words for your action verb and objective element. Use a thesaurus to help you with these lists. Use combinations of words from each list and write down new statements that are either directly or indirectly suggested.

4. Explore the boundaries of your problem area using the "Why?" method. Ask "Why?" about a tentative problem definition and write down your response. Reframe this response in the form of another problem statement. Ask "Why?" about this second statement and write down your response to it. Continue this activity until your statements become so abstract and philosophical as to be impractical.

5. Look over what you have done so far and collect all the statements you have generated. If you can think of any other ways to redefine your problem, add these statements to your list. You now are finished with the divergent phase of problem-finding.

Review your data. The data you generated during fact-finding can be an invaluable source of stimulation. Briefly review all of these data, but concentrate upon the critical concerns and priorities you identified. As you look over this material, try to think of any new perspectives and new ways of stating your problem. If you think of any, write them down using the "IWWM?" format. For example, the data generated about the computer problem discussed in Chapter 7 might stimulate such redefinitions as:

1. IWWM the screen be increased in size?
2. IWWM the computer be made lighter in weight?
3. IWWM the computer run without an external power source?
4. IWWM magnetic damage to disks be prevented?

List ownership and action elements. Your perspectives about a problem often can be expanded by considering a variety of ownership and action combinations. In other words, try looking at who else might be involved and what else might be done. Perhaps the easiest way to do this is to simply list, in two columns, ownership and action possibilities. For the computer problem (IWWM the computer be improved?), these lists might look like the following:

Potential Owners	Potential Actions
accountants	protect
software designers	prevent
students	provide

writers	increase
professors	decrease
musical composers	simulate
farmers	be made compatible
journalists	use
playwrights	perform
engineers	design

By examining different combinations of one word from each list, numerous problem redefinitions are suggested, such as:

1. IWWM musical composers perform scores before printing them?
2. IWWM playwrights simulate plays?
3. IWWM students use computers with others to solve problems?
4. IWWM engineers decrease design time?
5. IWWM software designers protect their work from pirates?

Use alternate words. The words you use initially to define a situation sometimes can act as blocks to creative thinking. Simply choosing one word over another very often can make a difference in how you view a situation. This method helps stimulate a variety of perspectives by using synonyms for key words or phrases in the original statement. For instance, two key words in the computer problem might be "improve" and "computer." Alternatives to these words could include:

Improve	*Computer*
better	processor
advance	calculator
revise	manipulator
promote	analyzer
correct	machine

Using different combinations of these words, redefinitions such as the following are suggested:

1. IWWM we revise a manipulator?
2. IWWM we correct a processor?
3. IWWM we promote a machine?
4. IWWM we advance a calculator?
5. IWWM we better an analyzer?

It should be apparent that these redefinitions are pretty abstract. As a result, you might not be satisfied with them in their present form. Instead, you probably will want to modify them. The best way to do this would be to use each definition as a stimulus for a more concrete statement. Thus, the concept of "correcting a processor" might suggest a problem of incorporating into internal memory some means for notifying the user when he or she has made an error in using the computer (although this may appear to be rather vague, so is my knowledge of computers!).

Use the "why" method. This techique is especially useful for exploring boundaries of problems and evaluating how abstract a statement is. In some cases, your initial statement will be either too concrete and specific or too abstract and philosophical. This can be avoided by considering a graduated range of potential definitions. Begin by asking "Why?" you want to do whatever is asked in your definition. Write down your response and use it to reframe the problem. Ask "Why?" again and repeat the process until your responses become highly abstract (if your initial statement is abstract, you will reach this point rather quickly).

As an example of the "why" method, consider the problem: IWWM I better organize my time? With this problem, you might proceed as follows:

Ask why: Why do I want to organize my time better?

Answer: To accomplish more work.

Redefine: IWWM I accomplish more work?

Ask why: Why do I want to accomplish more work?

Answer: To get paid more.

Redefine: IWWM I get paid more?

Ask why: Why do I want to get paid more?

Answer: To save for my retirement.

Redefine: IWWM I save for more retirement?

Ask why: Why do I want to save for my retirement?

Answer: To have money for food, shelter, and clothing.

Redefine: IWWM I have money for food, shelter, and clothing?

Ask why: Why do I want to have money for food, shelter, and clothing?

Answer: To be happy.

Redefine: IWWM I be happy?

As you can see, this method takes a problem and expands its perspective to a broad, abstract level. During convergence, you would review all of the redefinitions and select those that most appeal to you. Thus, in the example, you might decide that your "real" problem is to develop strategies for retirement saving. Getting paid more may be a subproblem for you that also would require your attention.

When using the "why" method, you might want to experiment with different answers to the various "why" questions. A slightly different response could suggest a fruitful perspective for viewing your problem. If you limit yourself to only one response per question, your redefinitions will be restricted in both quantity and quality. Thus, you might try using this procedure more than once.

The "why" method may not help you with all of your problems. However, it is a relatively easy and time efficient way to check on any erroneous assumptions you might make about a problem's boundaries. You should check such assumptions during problem-finding and not after you have started generating ideas (although you can recycle if required).

Review and redefine. As a final divergent step during problem-finding, look over all of the redefinitions you have generated. Without evaluating any of these statements, use them as stimulators for additional statements. When you think you have listed every possible redefinition, push yourself to list two or three more. You now should be ready for the convergent phase of problem-finding.

CONVERGING

The primary purpose of convergence in problem-finding is to select the one problem statement that best captures the "real" problem you want to solve. Once you have selected this statement, you can begin generating potential solutions.

If the first three stages seem like a lot of work just to choose one statement, don't be too discouraged. What you have accomplished so far is not wasted. The data you have collected and the understanding you have gained about your general problem area should help you produce a high-quality solution. Moreover, the data you accumulated during these stages often are useful during later stages—either as idea stimulators or as criteria for selecting solutions.

As a preliminary convergent step, write down as least five problem statements that best capture the situation you would like to deal with. Do this without referring to the statements you generated previously. These statements then should become part of the "pool" of statements you consider during convergence. Although this preliminary step is like divergence, it also is convergent in that it may help you synthesize some of your previous thinking.

Convergence during problem-finding works pretty much the same way as in the other stages. Begin by selecting statements that capture your interest. These are "hits." Then, identify hits that seem to cluster together based upon some common theme. Hits with something in common are known as "relates." The groups formed by the relates are referred to as "hotspots." The final convergent activity is to develop a problem statement that captures the essence of each hotspot. You then should select one statement as a tentative problem to use during idea-finding. This final statement may be one of the statements you already generated. Or it may result from a synthesis of elements from two or more hotspots.

To illustrate convergence, consider the previously discussed problem area of improving computers. Although you should generate more redefinitions in actual practice, the ones used here will give you some sense of the activity involved. The nine definitions generated were:

1. IWWM the screen be increased in size?
2. IWWM the computer be made lighter in weight?
3. IWWM the computer run without an external power source?
4. IWWM magnetic damage to disks be prevented?
5. IWWM musical composers perform scores before printing them?
6. IWWM playwrights simulate plays?
7. IWWM students use computers with others to solve problems?
8. IWWM engineers decrease design time?
9. IWWM software designers protect their work from pirates?

In reviewing these statements, you might select numbers 2, 3, 4, 6, 7, and 9 as your hits. After examining your hits, you next might select relates—hits with some common element. In this case, you could use statements 2 and 3 as one group of relates, 6 and 7 as a second group, and statement 9 as a third "group." Note that when you form relates you are, in effect, forming a tentative statement. For instance, the "relate" involving statements 2 and 3 is one of a common element of hardware improvements.

The hotspots formed by your relates become stimuli for generating problem redefinitions. In this instance, the hotspot containing statements 2, 3, and 4 might suggest redefinitions such as: IWWM we make a computer more versatile? IWWM we make a computer more portable? IWWM we make a computer easier to use?

It also is possible that you might want to avoid thinking of relates and hotspots. Instead, you might limit your convergent activities to identifying hits and selecting one that best captures the problem you want to solve. Regardless of which statement you finally decide to use, be sure that it has the potential to generate a number of different ideas.

A problem that has a high potential to stimulate many ideas should possess several characteristics. Such a statement should: have clear ownership and objective elements, allow you to think immediately of many possible ideas, motivate you to deal with it, be free of criteria, be stated briefly and concisely, and represent the "essence" of the situation you want to resolve. If the statement you have selected satisfies these criteria, you probably can use it to begin generating ideas.

GUIDELINES FOR TRAINERS

For this stage, your primary task as a trainer/facilitator is to help your class learn the various divergent and convergent techniques. You also should spend some time discussing the importance of problem-finding and analyzing the structure of problem statements. However, the most important thing for you to do is encourage your class to practice the problem-finding process.

When talking about the importance of problem-finding, stress the need to test assumptions about problem situations. At one time or another, we all fail to test some key assumption. Invariably, we chastise ourselves for failing to see the "obvious." However, the "obvious" often is not so obvious—even to trained observers. Instead, we all must consciously determine if we have considered all possible perspectives. Problem-finding can help us do this.

The section on the structure of problem redefinitions also is important. However, don't spend too much time or emphasize too strongly the different elements of a problem statement. It is more important to concentrate upon the guidelines for writing statements. Of these, I have found that novices are most likely to include criteria, include more than one problem, and be too wordy. Have your class write a number of statements individually and then discuss them in small groups, paying particular attention to the guidelines. If possible, stress the positive when evaluating statements and try not to be overly critical.

Of the divergent techniques discussed, the "why" method will be useful when uncertainty exists about whether or not the "real" problem is being dealt with. However, the other techniques can be equally useful, depending upon the nature of the particular problem. You also should note that using a specific technique probably is not as important as considering a large number of redefinitions—no matter how they are generated.

SUMMARY

Through increased understanding provided by objective-finding and fact-finding, problem-finding helps locate the "real" problem. Problem-finding enables you to find the one problem that is most important to you at a particular time. Moreover, it will assist in productively focusing your efforts to generate the highest-quality ideas possible. Problem-finding forces you to consider a variety of problem perspectives and to test all assumptions you might make.

There are at least five major techniques you can use to facilitate problem-finding. You may not want to use all of these techniques for every problem. However, try to use as many as you can.

One basic divergent technique involves reviewing all the data you generated during fact-finding. You can use these data as stimuli for generating problem redefinitions. A second technique uses lists of ownership and action elements as stimuli for problem statements. Developing alternate words and phrases for action verbs and objectives is a third way to stimulate new statements. A fourth method is to explore problem boundaries using the the "why" technique. With this approach, you continually reframe your problem until it becomes too abstract to be useful. Finally, you can stimulate redefinitions by reviewing all the statements you have generated and thinking of any other perspectives you might have overlooked.

Convergence during problem-finding is designed to help select the one statement that best captures your view of the problem. Begin by choosing "hits" or statements that have solution potential. Next, identify hits that cluster together based upon some common theme or bond. These hits with something in common are known as "relates." Clusters of relates, in turn, are known as "hotspots." After reviewing the hotspots, try to develop one final (but tentative) problem redefinition.

The final statement you select should: possess clear ownership and ob-jective elements, have the potential to stimulate many ideas, motivate you to deal with it, be free of criteria, be stated briefly and concisely, and represent the "essence" of the problem you want to solve.

Trainers should discuss the importance of problem-finding in relation to the CPS process. In particular, the need to test assumptions should receive special emphasis. Analyzing the structure of statements also is important but should not be overdone or overworked. More time should be devoted to practicing problem-finding than analyzing what it is.

When practicing generation of problem statements, be aware of the tend-ency of many people to include criteria and develop wordy statements that often contain more than one problem. Above all, don't let the class become overly concerned with learning the specifics of every divergent and con-vergent technique. The primary problem-finding activity involves gener-ating as many high-quality problems as possible and choosing one for idea-finding. How this statement is selected is not important. What is important is that the best possible statement be selected.

9
Idea-Finding: Individual Techniques

Once you decide to start idea-finding, you should have a good understanding of your general problem situation. You should feel comfortable with the redefinition you have selected. And some ideas already should be popping about in your head. If you have been impatient to start generating ideas, now is your chance.

Of all the CPS stages, more techniques exist for facilitating idea-finding than any other stage (VanGundy, 1981). Unfortunately, many of these techniques have been underutilized. As a result, a potentially valuable resource has been overlooked. The more aids you can draw upon to stimulate ideas, the more ideas you will be able to generate. And, if you can think of a lot of ideas, the odds are increased that at least one idea will solve your problem.

Because of the large number of idea-generation methods, they will be discussed in two chapters. Individual techniques will be described in this chapter and techniques designed for group use will be described in Chapter 10. Some of the factors involved in choosing between individual and group methods will be presented in this chapter. You also can use these factors as a guide for choosing idea-finding techniques.

OVERVIEW

Divergence during idea-finding is simply a matter of generating as many ideas as possible for solving your problem. Before doing this, however, decide if you need to use individual or group techniques. As shown in Figure 9–1, first "purge" yourself of all ideas you can think of "off the top of your head." Write them down as quickly as you can. Next, consider

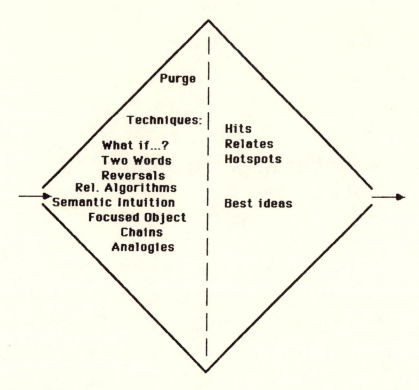

Figure 9–1
Idea-Finding: Individual Techniques

using one or more techniques to help prompt ideas. Guide your divergence by the four rules of brainstorming. For instance, it is vitally important that you avoid all criticism during divergence and try to list as many ideas as you can.

The convergent phase of idea-finding is similar to that of the other CPS stages. To narrow down the ideas you have generated, identify hits, relates, and hotspots. Then, select what you consider to be the best of the ideas that remain.

INDIVIDUAL VERSUS GROUP TECHNIQUES

One basic difference between individual and group techniques is that all individual techniques can be used by groups, but not all group techniques can be used by individuals. A group can modify any individual method and use it to generate ideas. However, most group methods were designed with groups in mind. Most of these techniques require at least three people and often five or more. However, there are several group methods that don't rely upon interaction with others and they easily can be adapted for individual use.

A major question about individual and group methods concerns how to select one approach over another. There obviously are advantages and disadvantages in both. However, neither individual nor group methods are "better." The issue revolves around the most appropriate conditions for using each.

According to Vroom and Yetton (1973), you should use individuals when: there is little time available, acceptance of your ideas by others is not important, and a high-quality solution is not important—that is, there are several possible solutions, any one of which will resolve the problem. The rationale behind these factors should be obvious. Using groups generally will consume more time than generating ideas by yourself. Acceptance of your ideas will be problematic only if others are affected by the problem. And a high-quality solution will be more likely when many minds can be brought to bear upon a problem.

There also are other factors about groups you should consider (Van-Gundy, 1984). First, the good news:

1. Groups have the potential advantage of being able to generate more ideas—in the same time period—than one individual working alone. As a result, the final solution should be of higher quality.

2. Groups also help satisfy social interaction needs of people. Many people would rather work with others than work alone.

3. Finally, groups have the potential to create a climate conducive to a high level of creative thinking. Individuals in groups have the potential to "spark" each other and stimulate a greater quantity and quality of ideas than individuals working alone.

There's an old saying that, "The best committee consists of two people, one of whom is absent." Although not everyone may agree with this, there are certain disadvantages to using verbally interacting groups. For example:

1. Some groups create a climate that is detrimental to creative thinking. For instance, continual criticism of each idea as it is proposed can create much frustration and dissatisfaction. As a result, most ideas produced will be mundane and low in quality.

2. Interpersonal conflicts can arise in groups, inhibit freedom of thought, and put a damper on the playful attitude needed to generate creative ideas.

3. Groups consume more time than individuals. If a solution is needed in a hurry, a group might not be able to help. There are exceptions, of course. However, these mostly involve well-trained groups facilitated by a skilled leader.

4. Some group members exert pressure to conform that disrupts the creative process. "Breakthrough" ideas will be more difficult to produce under such circumstances.

5. Dominant group members who attempt to take charge can cause se-

rious problems within groups if the attempts are not perceived as useful. Such domination can reduce participation by other group members. Thus, a serious imbalance in participation can develop. Not all group members will have an opportunity to contribute and their potential as a group resource is lost or not used fully.

Although these disadvantages may appear to be rather severe, there are ways to overcome them. For example, a skilled group leader can do much to smooth and sustain the idea-generation process. And there are certain types of group techniques that help reduce or eliminate some negative effects. More will be said on this matter in Chapter 10.

GUIDELINES FOR IDEA-FINDING

The following guidelines should help make divergence more successful. They are the four principles of brainstorming (Osborn, 1963):

1. Defer all judgment. Do not criticize your own ideas or the ideas of others. Save your analytical thinking for convergence. This is a very difficult guideline to follow—either as an individual or as a group. However, it must be followed if you want to generate a variety of ideas to consider later on.

2. Generate as many ideas as you can. "Quantity breeds quality," as Osborn used to say. The more ideas you think of, the greater the probability that at least one will be a winner. If you spend most of your time picking over only a few ideas, some high-potential ideas may be overlooked.

3. The wilder your ideas are, the better. Don't be restrained by what you consider to be "good" or "bad" ideas. There is no such thing during divergence. Even what initially appears to be a silly idea may prove to be useful later on. Some "off the wall" ideas can be modified to be more practical. Or, if modification isn't possible, such ideas frequently can stimulate more practical ideas.

4. Try to combine ideas. "Hitchhike" or "piggyback" upon others' ideas. In the case of individual divergence, try to build upon your own ideas. What else can you add? How might you combine the parts or concepts of two ideas into an even better idea?

Before you do any brainstorming, review these guidelines and make sure you understand them. Then, follow them! If you want to "cheat" and ignore one or two guidelines, be sure you do your cheating on the last two. The first two guidelines are the most important. Without deferring judgment, you will have trouble generating a large number of ideas. And, if you have trouble doing this, you will limit your final solution options.

In working with a number of groups, I usually can predict how successful a group will be in generating useful ideas based upon their adherence to the brainstorming rules. For instance, I recently worked with two groups on a general industrial problem. One group was very careful not to judge ideas and appeared to be having fun just writing down one idea after the other.

Several members of the second group, in contrast, were more concerned with criticizing every idea than with generating ideas (despite all my admonishments, they insisted on doing things their way). In fact, they seemed to be on a crusade to demonstrate how well they could tear down an idea. After 45 minutes, the first group had generated well over 75 ideas, while the first group was working on their seventh idea!

In a follow-up with the company several months later, I learned that more ideas from the first group were put into practice. And, as judged subjectively by a key manager, more ideas from this group were going to have a higher financial payoff for the company.

DIVERGING

The primary purpose of divergence during this stage is to generate as many ideas as possible. To begin, write down all the ideas you can think of at the moment. This is known as a "purge," since it will help you get rid of conventional and relatively trivial ideas first. If you are lucky, you also might come up with some high-potential ideas.

After you have completed your purge, consider using several idea-stimulation techniques. If you are motivated and have the time, try using all the techniques discussed in this chapter. Doing so will help acquaint you with the variety of methods available. It also will give you some idea of how different approaches can be used to prompt ideas. For instance, some of the methods rely upon components of the problem to stimulate ideas, while others use stimuli unrelated to the problem.

None of these techniques is guaranteed to prompt ideas. The final result will be a combined product of your personality, motivation, knowledge of the problem, and how you respond to a particular technique. Your experience in practicing with the methods, however, will help you determine which ones will work best for different types of problems.

The eight techniques that follow are presented roughly according to the extent to which they use unrelated stimuli. The first few methods use stimuli related to the problem, while the others rely more upon unrelated problem stimuli. Thus, if you are not familiar with idea-finding techniques, you should feel more comfortable with the first few methods. However, you should be able to master all the techniques with a little practice.

What if? This is a very basic yet potentially powerful technique. It is based upon a process you probably use quite often. All you do is ask: "What if?" in a sentence directed toward some aspect of your problem. To help think of some questions, consider what you would like to happen. Then, after listing a number of questions, use them as stimuli for ideas.

For example, suppose your problem is: "IWWM we reduce employee absenteeism?" Some sample "What if?" statements might be:

- What if no one was ever absent from work?
- What if employees couldn't wait to get to work?
- What if employees begged to work longer hours?
- What if employees were never sick?
- What if employees could take care of personal business while on the job?
- What if employees were always absent for legitimate reasons?
- What if employees found a suitable substitute to do their jobs whenever they were absent?
- What if employees became managers and docked their own pay every time they took an unauthorized absence?
- What if employees thought of their work as play?
- What if employees would automatically die after they took too many unauthorized absences?

After reviewing these statements, the followng ideas might be suggested:

1. Start an organization-wide program to encourage higher attendance.
2. Give a bonus to employees who have no unauthorized absences during a certain period of time.
3. Allow employees to work overtime when they want (if no logistical problems are created) and count this time toward leaves of absence.
4. Give employees extra sick time for not being absent within a certain time period.
5. Try flexible working hours (employees schedule their own hours before and after a specified "core" period).
6. Allow an employee council to reward and/or punish other employees for absences.
7. Where appropriate, allow certain employees to work at home.

One secret to the success of this method is to try for really wild "What if?" statements. Some statements can be practical, but most should be more in the area of fantasy.

Don't worry about being practical when you use a technique. The final product, of course, should be practical. However, the means used to achieve this product are irrelevant as long as you get the solution you need.

Two words. As discussed in Chapter 8, problem statements used in CPS contain an invitational stem (IWWM?), an ownership component, an action element, and a goal or objective area. If you have trouble thinking of ideas, it often can be traced to your choice of words for the action element and the goal statement. The meaning you give to certain words can block creative thinking just as much as a repressive organizational climate can.

However, blocks produced by word choices can be overcome. A simple way to do this is to substitute different words.

As described by Olson (1980; see also VanGundy, 1983), this is how the "two words" technique works:

1. Select two key words or phrases (usually the action verb and the objective) from the problem statement.

2. List alternate words for each of the words (a thesaurus or dictionary can help do this).

3. Select the first word from the first list and combine it with the first word from the second list.

4. Examine this combination and see if it suggests any ideas. If so, write them down.

5. Combine the first word from the first list with the second word from the second list.

6. Continue combining words from the two lists and writing down ideas until you have examined all possible combinations.

To illustrate this method, I again will use the problem of reducing employee absenteeism. The two key words I select are "reduce" and "absenteeism." These words seem to capture the essential nature of the problem. Next, I generate alternate meanings for these words as follows:

Reduce	*Absenteeism*
diminish	out
decrease	away
shorten	not in
curtail	not present
lessen	lacking
contract	missing

Finally, I compare different combinations (one from each list) and look for ideas. In this instance, the following types of ideas are suggested:

1. Design on absenteeism program in which employees are given so many days per year for "no excuse needed" absences (diminish/not in).

2. Survey employees to find what might be lacking in the workplace to cause them to be absent (decrease/lacking).

3. Lower the penalty for unauthorized absences if the absence was for less than a day (shorten/out).

4. Allow employees to be absent a specified number of days during a given quarter if they make up for them during the next quarter (curtail/away).

5. Offer employees the opportunity for self- or professional-development programs on the job. This might increase their motivation and decrease the number of absences (less/lacking).

Don't be too concerned about the particular key words or alternate meanings you use. Any combination that provides a different perspective on the problem will be useful.

Reversals. Many law enforcement agencies across the country have been using a rather ingenious approach to catching criminals. Although there are many variations to this approach, the basic elements are similar: Invite known felons to attend a party. Tempt them with prizes. Even offer to provide transportation. Then, once you have them together, arrest them.

This "sneaky" approach to catching criminals is a perfect example of the reversals method. The primary premise is: Instead of going out to catch the criminals, have the criminals come to you. In other words, reverse the traditional way of viewing law enforcement.

You can apply this procedure to generate ideas to many problems. Reverse the elements in your problem statements in as many ways as you can. Then, examine each reversal for possible ideas. For instance, consider the problem: IWWM we encourage people to wear seatbelts? You could reverse this statement in a number of ways:

1. IWWM we encourage people not to wear seatbelts?
2. IWWM we discourage people from wearing seatbelts?
3. IWWM people encourage themselves to wear seatbelts?
4. IWWM seatbelts be encouraged to wear people?
5. IWWM seatbelts be discouraged from wearing people?

In looking over these reversals, it should be evident that they don't need to be "logical." In fact, the more illogical they are the more likely it is that they will suggest a unique idea. Thus, the reversal of encouraging seatbelts to wear people might prompt the idea of seatbelts that automatically attach themselves to the wearer (such as is done in some new model cars).

The important thing about this method is that there is no "correct" way to do a reversal. Change any and all elements in your problem and hope you get a new perspective.

Relational algorithms. Much of what is involved in creative thinking involves playing with words. When you generate ideas, you manipulate words by trying them out in a variety of combinations. If one combination of words doesn't spark an idea, another one might.

The relational algorithms method (Crovitz, 1970) helps stimulate ideas by using two key words or phrases from a problem statement and a set of 42 "relational" words. However, this method does not use alternate word meanings to suggest ideas as done with the two words technique. Instead, you insert each relational word between the two key words. Then, you examine the combination to see what new ideas might be suggested.

The 42 relational words originally used by Crovitz and 19 prepositions I subsequently added (VanGundy, 1981) are:

about	below	near	then
above	beneath	not	though
across	beside	now	through
after	between	of	throughout
against	beyond	off	till
along	but	on	to
amid	by	opposite	toward
among	down	or	under
and	during	out	up
around	except	over	upon
as	for	past	when
at	from	round	where
because	if	since	while
before	in	still	with
behind	into	so	within
			without

Suppose your problem is: IWWM our organization improve internal communications? In this example, the key words you select might be "improve" and "communications." Inserting each of the relational words between these words might result in such ideas as:

1. Distribute reading material on how to improve communications (about).
2. Decrease possible misunderstandings by decentralizing decision making (above).
3. Design a formal feedback program to keep everyone well informed (around).
4. Develop a training program that uses role-playing exercises (between).
5. Increase the amount of upward communication (up).

When using this method, don't try too hard to develop ideas. Write down whatever ideas might be sparked. You never may find a logical connection among any of the word combinations. That's not what you should be looking for. Instead, let your thoughts flow and play around with any concepts suggested by a combination. In some cases, you even may want to use visualization.

Semantic intuition. This technique is one of many idea-generation aids developed at the Battelle Institute in Frankfurt, Germany (Schaude, 1979). An interesting feature of this method is its reversal of a procedure normally followed in many creative fields. That is, instead of generating ideas and assigning names to the resulting inventions, this procedure generates names and uses them to prompt ideas.

To use this procedure, select two areas related to the problem. Lists several words associated with each area. Then, examine different combinations of word pairs (one from each list) and write down any ideas stimulated.

To illustrate, I'll use the problem: IWWM we improve video productions in the training field? Two sets of words from this problem are: aspects of video productions and the topics dealt with by such productions. Words listed for each area might include:

Production Aspects	Training Topics
film	sales
camera	conflict
office setting	teamwork
screen	management development
lighting	job training
sound	leadership
dialog	time management
script	decision making
actors	creativity

Some ideas from different word combinations are: have groups view video tapes of their decision making efforts and suggest improvements (film/decision making), use special effect filters to show how people view the same situation differently (camera/conflict), secretly film an efficient video crew to illustrate good teamwork (screen/teamwork), design an abstract film that uses different degrees of light intensity to illustrate interpersonal conflict (lighting/conflict), design a job training script by recording informal job training discussions (dialog/job training), and illustrate creative problem solving by using a case study to demonstrate how some forms of creativity cannot be scripted in advance (script/creativity).

Focused-object. As described by Whiting (1958), this technique uses the principle of forced relationships to generate ideas. That is, two elements are "forced" together with the hope that their combination will suggest something new. With this method, however, one of these elements must be unrelated to the problem.

Suppose that your company is interested in ways to improve customer service (IWWM we improve customer service?). To use the focused-object method, you first would select some object unrelated to the problem. For example, you might select a bathroom sink. Next, describe the sink in some detail. Thus, you might say that it is porcelain, white, smooth, has a drain, faucet, and two water control knobs, hair collects in the drain and must be cleaned out periodically, a stopper allows the sink to retain water, it can mix hot and cold water, and requires regular cleaning. Using these descriptions as stimulators, write down any ideas suggested. In this case, you might think of such ideas as: a formal customer service representative (smooth), regular surveys of customer satisfaction (hair collects in drain), routine meetings with representative groups of customers (regular cleaning), appointing people to handle specific problems and follow through to resolution (hot and cold knobs), and using company line and staff personnel on a rotating basis to respond to customer problems (stopper retains water).

If you look at the descriptors I used to think of the ideas, a "logical" connection might not be apparent. For instance, the idea of rotating company personnel to function temporarily as customer service representatives was stimulated by a sink stopper. This particular item might stimulate any number of different ideas. However, for me and this particular problem, it caused me to think of the concepts of keeping and retaining. These then led me to the notion of remaining within the company which, in turn, stimulated the idea directly. Of course, how the stimulators work for you may be entirely different.

Attribute-association chains. We sometimes aren't fully aware of how our ideas originate. They somehow just seem to pop into our heads after we play around with the problem a bit. We often consciously or subconsciously free associate with our thoughts. That is, one idea leads to another and so on until we think of one that seems to work. Such a process usually is less than systematic.

A more efficient way to free associate is to use attributes of the problem. Attribute-association chains (VanGundy, 1983) does just that. To use this technique, list all of a problem's major attributes. Next, list all the subattributes you can think of. Then, free associate with each subattribute. For instance, if wood was one of the words, you might list: hard, grain, cereal, milk, drink, and thirsty. Finally, use each free association word as a stimulus for ideas.

To illustrate this technique, suppose your problem is: IWWM we improve an overhead projector? The major attributes might be listed as follows: lens, mirror, light, fan, and projection. Subattributes and free associations for each then might be listed:

lens—glass, see, ocean, waves, swim, tub, wash
mirror—Alice, wonderland, silly, cat, eyes, glance
light—bright, shine, chrome, bumper, repel, shock
fan—cool, ice, skate, bonfire, woods, leaves
projection—throw, baseball, strike, match, stick, crooked

Finally, each free association is examined for possible idea stimulation. In this instance, the following types of ideas might be suggested: build in a small viewing screen to preview a transparency (see), use a transparent, protective cover to prevent the projector glass from being scratched (tub), give human names to different projector models to stimulate sales (Alice), design projectors in the shape of animals to encourage children to use them for educational presentations (cat, eyes), install computer graphics that show a catalog of transparencies (glance), attach special padding around the projector bottom to protect it from bumping and dropping (bumper), use an automatic feed for transparencies (bonfire), and make a projector disposable and lightweight (throw, match).

Analogies. The analogies technique is one of the most powerful idea-generation methods. It has been used to solve numerous scientific problems and to generate many new consumer products. When used properly, analogies can be a rich source of ideas for resolving almost any type of problem.

The basic principle underlying analogies is that new perspectives on a problem can be gained by freeing yourself from familiar patterns. If you are too close and familiar to a problem, you are not likely to think of unique ways of viewing it. As a result, your ideas for resolving it may be mundane and common. The analogies technique helps to overcome this obstacle by allowing you to take a temporary "vacation" from your problem.

Taking a vacation from your problem is simply a matter of considering what else is like your problem. Then, select one of these comparisons, describe it in detail, and use your descriptions as idea stimulators. If you want, select another comparison and repeat the process to benefit from additional stimulators.

There are at least four major guidelines for using analogies. First, use animate analogies if your problem involves inanimate objects and inanimate analogies if your problem involves living things. Thus, if your problem is a "people" problem, select an analogy involving nonliving things. Second, when generating analogies, concentrate upon the major concept or principle underlying your problem. For instance, the problem of improving an overhead projector was concerned with the general issue of changing something for the better. Or reducing interpersonal conflict would be a general problem of making something less or smaller. Third, use analogies that involve considerable action. A good analogy should have a "life of its own" (de

Bono, 1970). Finally, don't be too constrained when thinking of your analogies. Wild and "off the wall" analogies usually work best.

Using analogies to generate ideas involves more than simply thinking about what else is like your problem. Following certain steps can help increase the value of the method considerably. To illustrate, I'll use the problem: IWWM we increase the employee retention rate?

The first step is to generate a list of analogies. For this problem, the underlying concept is one of people retention. Thus, the analogies should involve retention of inanimate things. Preface your search by stating: "Increasing the employee retention rate is like. . . . " Some potential analogies include:

- reinforcing a dam with additional earth or concrete
- adding layers of clothing to keep warm
- installing a wire grid to reinforce a concrete floor
- using a second paper plate with a hot picnic meal
- chemically spraying trees to increase their survival rate
- building an earthen retaining wall in front of your house

Try to generate at least five analogies during this step.

Next, select one of these analogies and elaborate upon it. Select one that you can describe in some detail. It is important that you use as much detail as you can and include many "action" types of statements. Don't just list single words that are involved. For instance, with the spraying example, you might elaborate upon it as follows:

- Coverage should be thorough, covering all tree surfaces.
- You must be careful not to kill other plant life.
- Spraying requires uses of an airplane for large-scale application.
- Growth progress should be checked periodically.
- Large trees are pruned to permit smaller trees to grow.
- Technicians walk among the trees for close inspections.
- Dead or diseased trees should be removed.
- Some healthy trees need to be harvested periodically.

When generating these descriptors, don't be overly concerned about technical accuracy. Being "correct" about some particular fact is less important than generating as much information as you can. The primary purpose of this step is to create as much stimulus material as possible.

The final step in using analogies is to focus again upon the original problem ("coming home" from your "vacation"). Using each descriptor as a stimulator, write down any ideas you can think of. Just remember not to use any evaluation. Idea quality is not important during this activity.

For this example, you might come up with such ideas as: ensure that all employees feel they are treated equally and receive equal attention (thorough coverage), provide incentives to stay with the company for so many years (be careful not to kill other plant life), award airplane vacations for meritorious retention records (requires airplane), allow employees greater choice of job assignments (requires airplane), require managers to maintain more personal contact with employees and take a greater interest in personal problems (check growth progress), conduct regular, informal job attitude surveys (check growth progress), strengthen early retirement incentives to promote more junior personnel (large trees pruned), reward upper-level managers for spending more time "walking the floor" and talking with employees (close inspections), improve employee health benefits (diseased trees removed), and give more authority and responsibility to lower-level employees (harvest healthy trees).

CONVERGING

Convergence during idea-finding involves looking for hits, relates, and hotspots. If you have little time or an exceptionally large number of ideas, it is possible to simplify the convergence process. Select what you consider to be the one or two most important criteria and use them as guides to eliminate many of the ideas. For instance, you might eliminate all those ideas that cost more than a certain amount or require more time than is available. However, use caution with this approach. You don't want to eliminate an idea that has the potential to be modified into something more workable.

To begin convergence, identify what you consider to be the most promising ideas (hits). Keep in mind that ideas are solutions in the rough. You don't have to accept an idea as is. You can modify it or combine it with other ideas. Next, examine all of your chosen hits and identify relates. That is, look for common themes and similarities among the hits. One caution: Don't force together a cluster of ideas just to form a relate. Some ideas may need to stand alone. Finally, select the relates (and any single ideas) that seem to have the most promise for resolving your problem (hotspots). If necessary, modify any ideas to form the best possible solutions.

You now should have selected at least three potential solutions. However, if you plan to use group idea-finding, you should move on to Chapter 10. Otherwise, you now are ready for solution-finding (Chapter 11).

GUIDELINES FOR TRAINERS

Deciding between individual and group idea-generation techniques usually is not difficult. Practical constraints often dictate the choice. If little time is available or a group is not available, for example, then individual ideation is the only option. However, there also are many instances in which groups can be beneficial. As a trainer, you should ask your class to discuss some of the advantages and disadvantages involved in using groups.

The four brainstorming principles discussed in this chapter are very important. Class members should memorize them and practice using them whenever possible. It is especially important that they practice deferring judgment. Although this chapter is concerned with individual methods, group practice can facilitate learning this principle.

One simple exercise to introduce the importance of deferred judgment requires two groups. Before discussing this principle, place each group in a different location, out of earshot of the other. Tell both groups to work on some general problem such as: IWWM we reduce the number of drunk drivers? Instruct one of the groups in the four brainstorming principles. Emphasize the need to withhold all criticism. Ask a member of this group to function as a monitor to enforce this principle.

Don't mention anything to the other group other than the problem. Give both groups about 10 minutes to come up with as many ideas as they can. After this time, reconvene the groups and have them total up their ideas. In most instances, the group following the brainstorming principles will generate a larger number of ideas. (You can mention how the odds also favor higher-quality ideas when a large number is generated.) After discussing the results, note how the same principle can work equally well for individual idea generation.

When discussing idea-generation methods, I like to point out how such techniques can be a useful resource. Rather than relying upon our same routine approaches, a variety of methods can provide an increased amount of stimulation for prompting ideas. Because we have little to lose and a lot to gain, playing around with techniques is a low-cost way to solve problems.

You also might note that there is nothing magical about idea-generation methods. They are simply aids that can help some people with some problems. All of the techniques will not be equally useful for everyone. However, if only one technique works well for a problem, all experimentation will have been justified.

Like most anything else, learning to use the techniques in this chapter requires practice. To make them easier to learn, I have presented them roughly in order of how difficult they are to master. Not everyone will require such a progressive approach, but there is little to lose in following it.

As much as possible, I have organized the techniques according to how much unrelated stimulus material is used. That is, some methods generate ideas by using aspects of the problem, while others rely upon stimuli unrelated to the problem. Most people are more comfortable starting with related aspects.

One technique likely to cause some trouble for a few people is analogies. Although we all use analogies in much of our day-to-day problem solving, we may not be fully aware of what we are doing. Structuring the approach and making it systematic sometimes are confusing.

A major problem some people have is thinking of the analogies themselves. As I mentioned in the text, analogies are developed by thinking of the major concept or principle involved. Usually, this concept or principle is a more abstract or general restatement of the problem. Have your class spend some time practicing identification of these principles. Have them practice with several different types of problems involving both animate and inanimate things. Try the example in the text and have them develop their own examples. This is the only way they can learn how to apply this method appropriately.

Another point to discuss is the difficulty some people have in using unrelated stimuli to prompt ideas. If a "logical" connection is not apparent, the process involved can be difficult for some. You should stress that there is no "logical" way of using the stimuli. Rather, the stimuli help us play around with a problem and view it from different perspectives. In addition, such stimuli often can help gain access to many of the "hidden" ideas that float around in our minds—ideas we may not be fully aware of until they are prompted by something else.

SUMMARY

Divergent idea-finding techniques are designed for either individuals or groups. All individual methods can be used by groups, but not all group methods can be used by individuals. Among the advantages of using groups are: satisfaction of social interaction needs, a larger number of ideas can be generated when compared to a single individual, and a positive group climate can be motivating and result in an atmosphere conducive to creative thinking. Among the disadvantages of groups are: continual criticism of ideas can reduce idea quantity and create dissatisfaction, interpersonal conflicts can be counterproductive, groups can consume more time than individuals, pressures for conformity can reduce idea quality, and domination by one or more group members can lead to unequal participation.

Being able to use a large number of idea-generation methods will increase the odds that at least one will help stimulate high-quality ideas. Before using such methods to begin divergence, purge yourself of all ideas you can think of on the spot. Then, experiment with a variety of methods and find out which ones work best for you.

Divergence during idea-finding should be guided by the four principles of brainstorming: defer all judgment, generate as many ideas as you can, the wilder the ideas the better, and try to combine ideas. Among the many individual idea-finding techniques are: what if?, two words, reversals, relational algorithms, semantic intuition, focused-object, attribute-association chains, and analogies.

The convergent process during idea-finding is similar to that used during previous stages. First, look over all the ideas you have generated and identify hits. Then, look for relates—clusters of ideas with commonalities. Finally, select hotspots—clusters with the greatest potential to resolve your problem. If necessary, combine or modify any ideas. At the end of the idea-finding stage, you should have selected at least three ideas for further evaluation during solution-finding.

Trainers should encourage their classes to discuss the advantages and disadvantages of using group idea-finding methods. It is important that class members memorize the four brainstorming principles. An exercise in using the principles can vividly demonstrate their importance. Have one group follow the brainstorming principles and the other generate ideas as usual. Then, compare the results. The group that followed the principles should generate more ideas.

Analogies is a powerful method that a lot of people have trouble using appropriately. As a result, special emphasis should be given this method. Practice generating analogies by having class members practice identifying the basic concept underlying a problem. And be sure to stress the need to elaborate upon an analogy in detail using "action" phrases.

In general, trainers should note there is nothing "logical" about using unrelated stimuli to help prompt ideas. Such stimuli are intended as material to play around with. Idea generation is not a magical process. However, freeing the mind to be open to new methods is an important first step.

10
Idea-Finding: Group Techniques

Chapter 9 dealt with individual techniques for diverging during idea-finding. This chapter continues idea-finding, but discusses group techniques for divergence. The convergent process essentially is the same for both individuals and groups.

The factors involved in deciding between individual and group methods were discussed in Chapter 9. You should review this material if you have any questions.

Most idea-finding guidelines and principles apply to both individual and group methods. For instance, having a large number of methods to use increases the odds that a group will find several it can use successfully. Also, the four brainstorming principles outlined in Chapter 9 are equally important when using group techniques. Briefly, these principles are: defer all judgment when generating ideas, generate as many ideas as you can—quantity breeds quality, the wilder your ideas, the better, and try to combine ideas.

From my experiences in working with hundreds of groups over the years, I believe that group techniques are of secondary importance. Far more important are the type of individuals used, the climate that exists, and the skills of a group facilitator. (Although many of these factors already have been described, group facilitation skills will be discussed in Chapter 13.) Nevertheless, many deficiencies in group climate and leader skills can be overcome by using certain group techniques.

BRAINSTORMING VERSUS BRAINWRITING

In general, group idea-generation methods can be divided into brainstorming and brainwriting variations. The differences between these variations can be significant, especially when a skilled leader is not available. As a result, you should have a basic understanding of how these approaches differ. (For a comprehensive discussion of brainstorming and brainwriting methods, see VanGundy, 1984.)

Most people are familiar with brainstorming, particularly Osborn's (1963) approach. However, formal brainstorming differs considerably from what a lot of groups do. Many groups use brainstorming without following any brainstorming principles. I refer to this approach as unstructured brainstorming. In contrast, structured brainstorming groups follow the four brainstorming principles.

Structured brainstorming groups usually will produce more ideas than unstructured brainstorming groups. Groups using unstructured brainstorming typically spend so much time criticizing ideas and wandering from the task that they accomplish very little.

Brainwriting refers to a class of group methods in which the ideas are generated silently and in writing. Two major types of brainwriting are nominal and interacting (VanGundy, 1984). In nominal brainwriting, ideas are generated by individuals who do not share their ideas with other group members. By comparison, interacting brainwriting uses ideas that are shared with other group members.

Brainstorming and brainwriting approaches have certain strengths and weaknesses that tend to balance each other. Neither approach is better than the other. Deciding between the two is a matter of deciding which trade-offs you are willing to accept.

Major brainstorming strengths include accommodation of social interaction needs, potential for high cohesiveness, and stimulation by the ideas of others. Although a skilled group leader and a trained group can help overcome many brainstorming weaknesses, there are potential liabilities. For example, brainstorming can be counterproductive when interpersonal conflict exists, when one or more members dominate the discussion, when status differences inhibit some members' participation, and when pressures to conform lead to low-quality solutions.

Major advantages of brainwriting include elimination of domination, interpersonal conflict, and status differences. Brainwriting also helps ensure greater task orientation, provides a ready-to-use written record of ideas, and, under certain conditions, produces more ideas than brainstorming. On the down side, brainwriting is unattractive to some because it tends to eliminate social interaction. It also contributes little to group cohesion. This latter liability can be serious in new groups or in groups where a climate conducive to creativity is lacking. Developing a positive climate requires some verbal interaction.

The obvious solution to the advantages and disadvantages of these approaches it to use both. As long as you have enough time and consider the problem to be important, try to use at least one technique from each approach. In addition to offsetting the disadvantages of brainstorming and brainwriting, a different format also might help spark unique ideas. Simply doing something differently can provide new perspectives. If you always use brainstorming, then you may find yourself in a rut—even if a skilled leader is used and the members are well trained.

OVERVIEW

Divergence during group idea-finding is similiar to individual idea generation. The objective is to generate as many ideas as possible. However, groups can use some techniques not available to individuals working alone. As with individual idea generation, groups should follow the four brainstorming rules and be especially careful to avoid any criticism.

Convergence during group idea-finding also is similar to convergence during individual idea-finding. Groups should identify hits, relates, and hotspots. Then, they should select the best of the ideas for consideration during solution-finding.

Figure 10–1 illustrates the divergent and convergent phases for group idea-finding. Six brainstorming and four brainwriting methods are described in this chapter. Classical brainstorming, the SIL method, and the Gordon/Little technique are traditional brainstorming approaches. Picture stimulation, greeting cards, and super heroes, however, require a more playful attitude than the other brainstorming methods. In many situations, these latter methods can be more fun to use and more productive (in terms of generating unique ideas). Three of the four brainwriting techniques (pin cards, brainwriting pool, and method 6–3–5) are variations of the same general procedure. The fourth brainwriting approach, collective notebook, is intended for organization-wide idea generation.

BRAINSTORMING TECHNIQUES

Classical Brainstorming. Originally developed by Alex Osborn (1963) about 40 years ago, classical brainstorming is the most widely known creative problem solving technique. Most people probably are not aware of how Osborn conceived brainstorming. In addition to following the four principles outlined previously, there are several relatively unknown features.

Osborn viewed brainstorming as a process—not just a technique. As discussed in Chapter 2, Osborn described brainstorming as involving the stages of fact-finding, idea-finding, and solution-finding. Because brainstorming eventually evolved into CPS, the other stages will not be discussed in this chapter. Instead, the focus will be upon the idea-finding phase of brainstorming.

The key to a successful brainstorming session is preparation. Prior to a

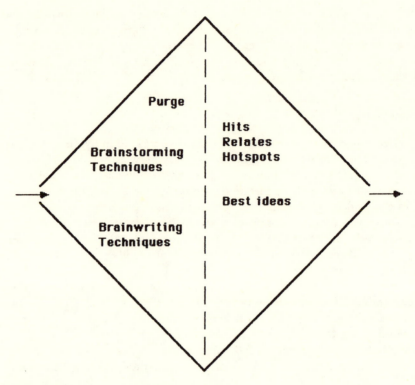

Figure 10–1
Idea-Finding: Group Techniques

session, participants should be sent a problem statement, background information, a copy of the brainstorming rules, and information on the time and location of the session. At the session, groups should be limited to 6 to 12 people (I have found 5 or 6 to be an ideal number). They should be instructed in the general procedures involved, redefine the problem if necessary, and participate in a warmup exercise (e.g., different uses for a brick).

The leader should write the problem on a chalkboard or flip chart. Group members suggest ideas by raising their hands. A recorder then writes down all ideas mentioned. After 30 to 45 minutes, the session is ended. The ideas then are submitted for evaluation to another group, the same group, or someone with implementation responsibility.

To be successful, brainstorming groups must be led by a skilled leader (or the members must be experienced). Ideally, group members should receive some training and practice in brainstorming. However, if a skilled leader is not available and the members are not trained, the group will have to monitor itself. It is especially important that one or more members ensure that all evaluation of ideas is avoided during divergence. Otherwise, the group is likely to go off track with little to show for its efforts.

One trick used by some group leaders to keep a group on track is known as "sequencing" (Bouchard, 1972). Instead of raising hands to suggest ideas, group members verbalize their ideas one at a time by going around the group. Each person suggests his or her idea in sequence. If someone cannot think of an idea during their turn, they simply say "pass" and the next person suggests an idea. A major advantage of sequencing is that it helps ensure equal participation and neutralizes dominant group members.

SIL method. This technique was developed at the Battelle Institutes in Frankfurt, Germany (Warfield, Geschka & Hamilton, 1975). The letters SIL are a German language acronym that translates roughly as "successive integration of problem elements." The steps for using this approach are:

1. Individuals silently generate ideas in writing to a problem statement.

2. Two group members select one idea each and read it aloud.

3. The other group members verbally think of ways to combine these two ideas into one idea.

4. A third group member reads one of his or her ideas and the group attempts to integrate it with the one just generated.

5. The process of reading and integrating ideas continues until a workable solution is found or time expires.

Suppose that a group is dealing with a problem of ways to reduce scrap waste generated by a plant. After a period of individual divergence, two group members read one of their ideas aloud: develop a more efficient mold and assign a "waste monitor" to each work unit. Next, the other group members try to integrate these ideas. As with the individual techniques that rely upon forced relationships, the final product may not appear to be logical. Rather, the combination is valued more for its stimulus potential. In this example, the group might think of an idea such as "allow work units to decide how much waste is acceptable," or "develop flexible molds that can be adjusted by individual work units." Either of these ideas would be integrated with another idea and the process would continue. The group would stop once an acceptable idea is produced.

As you might guess, the "convergent" nature of this divergent technique can be a liability. By concentrating upon a specific set of ideas and progressively integrating them, the number of ideas considered will be limited. Moreover, having to combine all ideas discussed could weaken some otherwise high–potential ideas. On the other hand, the structured, task-oriented nature of this method will help keep the group on track.

Gordon/Little. This technique has high potential to produce unique ideas. However, the group members must not be aware of the problem.

To use this method, the leader first gradually reveals hints about the problem, beginning at a high level of abstraction. The hints become less abstract until the problem is revealed. As the leader provides each bit of problem information, the group members generate solutions to solve the problem described. After the problem is revealed to the members, they use all of their ideas as stimuli for potential solutions to the primary problem.

The Gordon/Little technique was developed by William Gordon while he worked at the Arthur D. Little consulting company (Taylor, 1961). Gordon noticed that many people have trouble solving problems because they are too close to them (much like the saying, "you can't see the forest for the trees"). When we are too familiar with a problem, obvious and trivial solutions often are the only ones we think of. However, once the problem is made "unknown" to us, whole new solution possibilities are opened up. As a result, idea originality usually increases as well.

This method requires some planning and a flexible leader. First, write down an abstract description of the problem. Suppose the primary problem is: IWWM we increase the number of employee parking spaces? The leader might restate this problem by asking the group to: "Think of ways to get more of something." After the group generates ideas for this problem, the leader would restate the problem in somewhat less abstract terms. For example: "Think of ways to enlarge an area." Following more idea generation in response to this problem, the leader then provides another, even less abstract problem. In this case, the problem might be: "Think of ways to obtain more space." Finally, the leader would reveal the primary problem and ask the group to use the ideas already generated as stimuli.

Picture stimulation. This technique has been referred to as visual synectics (Schaude, 1979) and more recently as picture projection group confrontation (Geschka, von Reibnitz & Storvik, 1981). One variation is known as Battelle Bildmappen brainwriting (Warfield, Geschka & Hamilton, 1975). I have chosen the name picture stimulation, since that reflects the primary principle involved.

This approach works especially well after a group has used classical brainstorming and wants more unique ideas. The idea stimuli in this method are obtained from pictures unrelated to the problem. The steps are:

1. Select a variety of pictures and place them on overhead transparencies, slides, or in notebooks given to individual group members. The pictures should not be too abstract and should contain a variety of action elements. *National Geographic* is an excellent source.

2. Group members examine one of the pictures and describe aloud—in detail—what they see. A recorder writes down the descriptions on a flip chart.

3. Group members look at each description and use it as a stimulus for suggesting ideas.

4. After finishing with one picture, another is selected and the process is repeated.

Groups using this method sometimes become embroiled in discussions about what is or is not shown in a picture. Avoid such discussions when possible. The correctness of the descriptions are not important. It is more important that the group has a variety of stimulation sources to use.

As an example of this approach, suppose you are a trainer conducting a career counseling workshop. The problem might be defined as: IWWM I improve my career options? For one of the pictures, I select a scene from the mountains in Mexico (VanGundy, 1983). There is a stream with white water, large rocks are piled along the shore, two mountains are located in such a way that a "V" shape is formed at their juncture, there are light, wispy clouds in the sky, and the color of the sky ranges from light blue at the bottom of the picture to dark blue at the top.

In addition to this information, I also might note that the water probably is cold, large stones on the shore will help prevent soil erosion, water pressure is higher at the bottom of the stream, fish might be swimming in the stream, the water looks too dangerous for boating, and the white water is caused by rocks under the surface.

Using all of these descriptions, the following ideas might be suggested:

1. Consider only one career objective at a time.
2. Develop a 1-, 5-, and 10-year career plan.
3. Make a list of strengths and weaknesses and use them to suggest possible job changes.
4. Examine job requirements that might lurk "below the surface."
5. Use visualization to picture yourself performing a variety of careers.
6. Don't become discouraged, since there will be many "hills and valleys" involved.
7. Talk to people in career fields that interest you.
8. Set a deadline for making a career change.
9. Assume that anything is possible and decide what you would like to do. Then, develop a plan to achieve it.
10. Consult a book that describes the full range of possible occupations.

Greeting cards. This method is based upon a creativity exercise originally developed by Pickens (1985) to illustrate the importance of playful thinking. After making a few minor changes, I modified it to serve as an idea-finding technique.

The steps involved are quite simple:

1. Pictures are cut from magazines, catalogs, and newspapers. Collect at least 10 pictures for each group of five people.

2. Groups paste the pictures ("glue sticks" work well for this purpose) onto folded pieces of paper to produce improvised greeting cards. Each card should convey some theme (e.g., birthdays, get well, anniversaries, friendship).

3. Groups study the cards they produced and those of other groups and use them as sources of idea stimulation. (The themes expressed in the cards as well as the pictures can be used as stimuli.)

A minor variation of this procedure involves having individuals develop their own greeting cards and sharing them with the other group members. Each card then would be used for idea stimulation. When more than one group is involved, another variation is to have the groups exchange their cards and use the exchanged cards to prompt ideas.

This technique helps liven a traditional brainstorming session. It works best with people who have a playful attitude. However, it also can create a climate conducive to creative thinking, which can help open up more "serious" people. The result often is several unique idea perspectives.

The idea stimulation mechanism involved is almost identical to that used in the focused-object technique (Chapter 9): An unrelated picture is used to prompt ideas. However, the greeting cards method also has an additional source of stimulation in the themes represented by the cards. Moreover, the climate produced by the playful attitudes required can further prompt creative ideas.

To illustrate this method, consider the problem: IWWM we make our staff meetings more efficient? A card is designed with pictures of boots. The caption reads, "If you don't write soon, I'll give you the boot!" Both the boots and the caption can be used to prompt ideas. Using the boots alone, the group might think of such ideas as: include only people who do not talk much (from how boots fit), develop an agenda and assign someone to ensure it is followed (from how boots sometimes are polished and maintained by others). The caption, on the other hand, might prompt such ideas as: use a mild electrical shock in the chair seat whenever someone talks too long (from the notion of "a kick in the seat of the pants") or conduct meetings by conference call (or computer networks) and turn off anyone who rambles out of control (from the concept of "kicking out").

Super heroes. Another approach for livening up a brainstorming session is super heroes (Grossman & Catlin, 1985). For people who like playful groups and for budding actors, this method should prove popular. By assuming the identity of various super heroes, group members increase the variety of perspectives they can use in approaching a problem. The basic procedure involved is: select one of the super heroes, assume that person's identity, and think of ideas from the super hero's perspective. A recorder writes down any ideas suggested.

Some examples of super heroes are:

1. Captain America: The symbol of all-American ideals (truth, justice, liberty, pursuit of happiness). A charismatic leader, he easily persuades others with his positive ideas. He is a super athlete with great strength. His Captain America shield can protect him from any harm.

2. Dr. Strange: A skilled magician and sorcerer. He is adept at creating illusions. He also has the ability to cure people, control people and situations, and bring about many changes and transformations. His only weakness is temporary lapses of concentration.

3. E-Man: He is pure energy and possesses an infinite amount of it. He can assume any form, but is affected by any weaknesses of the form he assumes. He normally sleeps in a toaster.

4. Nova Kane: An exotic dancer before becoming a super hero, she is the female counterpart of E-Man.

5. Spiderman: Has the ability to walk on walls and ceilings, swing through the air on his web, and capture people with his web. He can stick to any surface. A unique ability is his "spider sense" which warns him of any danger.

6. Wonder Woman: She is extremely strong, agile, and athletic. With her magic bracelets, she can deflect bullets and anything thrown at her. With her magic lasso, she can rope anything at an almost unlimited distance. When her lasso encircles someone, they are forced to tell the truth. She flies her own invisible airplane.

7. Mr. Fantastic: Known as Reed Richards in everyday life, he is the smartest man in the world. Mr. Fantastic can stretch any part of his body to any length. His body is completely pliable.

8. Invisible Girl (a.k.a. Susan S. Richards): Has the ability to make herself and other people and things invisible. She can make things reappear at will and can create invisible barriers for protection.

9. Superman: He is the strongest man on earth, has X-ray vision and can fly at will. He can be weakened only by Kryptonite, a remnant from the planet of his birth. He has appeared in several movies, wears sunglasses to bed, and recently moved from Metropolis to Los Angeles. Jumps off buildings whenever someone says, "Look. Up in the sky. . . . "

10. Batman: As millionaire Bruce Wayne, Batman uses his powers of sleuthing and deduction to solve heinous crimes. He and his friend Robin (the Boy Wonder) ride around in a Batmobile, Batcycle, Batplane, Batbat, and so on. He uses his cunning mind to outwit the criminal element.

11. The Human Torch: Known for his short temper and hot head, Johnny Storm (the Invisible Girl's brother) emits fire, controls fire, and can tolerate any degree of heat. He also can fly.

12. Impossible Man: Born on the planet Pop-Up, Impossible Man can change himself into any shape and material. The only problem is the loud popping sound he makes whenever he changes shape. He is a fun-loving person and is the most optimistic person in the world.

The most efficient way to use Super Heroes is to work with one character at a time. Each person should describe his or her character and any special powers, weaknesses, and so forth. Then, the entire group should use the descriptions as stimuli for brainstorming ideas. To add to the fun atmosphere, group members could put on costumes of the characters they represent.

As an illustration of how this method is used, someone portraying Spiderman could prompt a lot of ideas from the special web he uses. Or, the web might suggest the general notion of a network that could be applied to a variety of problems.

BRAINWRITING TECHNIQUES

Pin cards. This method is a simple alternative to brainstorming. It is especially useful whenever a skilled leader is not available, group members are not experienced and trained in brainstorming, one member dominates the discussion, or conflict exists between two or more members. It also will help ensure equal participation in idea generation by providing a relatively safe environment for shy or inhibited individuals. The result frequently is a greater quantity of ideas when compared to unstructured brainstorming. A diagram of the pin cards process is shown in Figure 10–2.

The basic steps are (Geshka, von Reibnitz & Storvik, 1981):

1. Five to eight people are seated around a small table.
2. Each person is given a stack of large cards (e.g., five-by-seven inch index cards or blank computer cards) and a pen or large marker.
3. One idea is silently written on each card and passed to the right.
4. The person receiving the card reads it and tries to think of any new ideas stimulated by the idea or ways to modify it.
5. New ideas are written down on another card and passed to the right.
6. This process of reading cards, writing down new ideas, and passing cards to the right is repeated until time is called (usually 20 to 30 minutes).
7. The cards are collected and "pinned" to a bulletin board or spread out on a large table. Categories can be used to organize the cards, such as by types of ideas or functional areas affected.
8. Group members look over the cards and silently write down any new ideas.

Brainwriting pool. The brainwriting pool method is similar to the pin cards technique. The primary difference is that written ideas are placed in a "pool" of other ideas. Someone else's ideas then are removed from the pool and used for stimulation of additional ideas (Figure 10–3). As with pin cards, no discussion is permitted during idea generation.

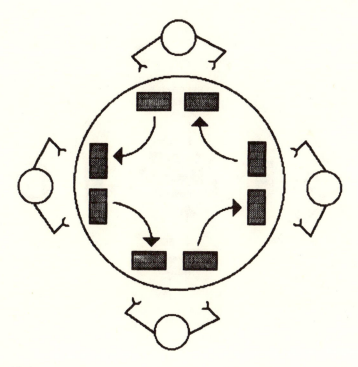

Figure 10–2
Pin Cards

The steps for using the Brainwriting Pool are (Geschka, von Reibnitz & Storvik, 1981):

1. A group of five to seven people are seated around a small table.
2. Each person silently writes four ideas on a sheet of paper and places the paper in the center of the table.
3. Someone else's paper is taken from the pool and the ideas written on it are used for stimulation of new ideas.
4. New ideas are silently written down on the paper (any number desired).
5. When additional stimulation is needed, the paper is exchanged for another one from the pool.
6. The process continues until time is called (usually after about 20 to 30 minutes).

A major advantage of the brainwriting pool over pin cards lies in the amount of discretion provided the group. When using pin cards, members are encouraged to keep the cards circulating. Brainwriting, in contrast, allows members to hold onto a sheet of paper for as long as they want (i.e., brainwriting pool users can determine their own "exchange rate").

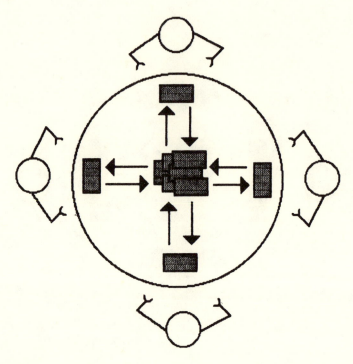

Figure 10–3
Brainwriting Pool

Method 6–3–5. There are several different versions of this method. The version described here is one of the first brainwriting techniques. It is used by having six people write down three ideas during five-minute intervals. The specific steps are (Warfield, Geschka & Hamilton, 1975):

1. Six people in a group each are given a form to record ideas (Figure 10–4).
2. Three ideas are silently written down in the first row on the form.
3. After five minutes have elapsed, the forms are passed to the right.
4. The first three ideas are read and used as stimulation for three new ideas, which are written down in the second row on the form.
5. After five minutes, the forms are passed to the right again and the process is repeated until all six rows have been completed. (The last column on the form can be used for evaluation ratings during convergence.)

Because of the way this method is structured, 108 ideas should be generated in 30 minutes. However, not all groups are able to produce this many ideas. Frequently, the time pressure results in fewer than three ideas during

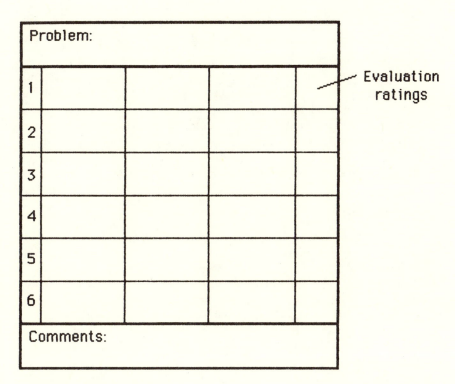

Figure 10–4
Method 6–3–5 Idea Form

each five-minute period. Thus, you might want to experiment with longer time periods.

Collective notebook (CNB). Haefele (1962) developed an organization-wide method for collecting ideas. In contrast to the brainwriting methods discussed previously, the collective notebook approach does not require face-to-face interaction. Instead, ideas are generated independently and collected later for evaluation.

The procedure for using CNB is as follows:

1. Preselected participants are provided with a notebook containing a problem statement.
2. Each participant writes down one idea per day for one month.
3. At the end of the month, participants develop a written summary, note their best ideas, and record any general comments or recommendations.
4. A coordinator collects the notebooks, categorizes the ideas, and prepares a written summary.

5. Participants individually review the summary and add any new ideas they might think of.

Pearson (1979) describes success in using a variation of the CNB approach. He had participants exchange their notebooks with one other person (who was preassigned) at the end of two weeks. As a result, stimulation by the ideas of others was possible.

Obviously, this method requires more time than the other group approaches. However, what it loses in spontaneous idea generation, it makes up for in the incubation period provided. The only negative feature is maintaining motivation of the participants over an extended period of time.

CONVERGING

The convergent process for group techniques is identical to that used for individual idea-finding: Identify hits, relates, and hotspots. Then, select the best ideas for additional evaluation.

If a group is dealing with a large number of ideas, they might do an initial screening to make the number of ideas more manageable. For instance, they might decide upon the two or three most important criteria and eliminate any ideas that fail to satisfy these criteria.

The rest of the convergent process involves selecting the most promising ideas (hits), identifying hits with common themes (relates), and selecting relates with the greatest potential for resolving the problem (hotspots). As with any convergent process, some ideas may need to be combined or modified. When the final set of ideas has been selected, the group can move on to solution-finding.

GUIDELINES FOR TRAINERS

Some people might consider at least three of the brainstorming methods in this chapter to be rather unusual. Classical brainstorming, the SIL method, and, to some extent, the Gordon/Little technique are fairly traditional. That is, the ideas are verbally generated in a relatively straightforward manner using conventional brainstorming principles.

In contrast, greeting cards and super heroes represent unorthodox approaches. They require the participants to engage in various "playful" activities before generating ideas. As a result, some people initially might feel uncomfortable using these methods. If this is the case with your class, introduce the other methods first. You also can explain how playfulness can create a climate highly conducive to creative thinking. However, don't force anyone to participate who would feel uncomfortable doing so.

When discussing and using the techniques in this chapter, the following guidelines might be helpful.

Classical brainstorming. Provide experience in using the sequencing procedure. Even experienced groups with a trained facilitator can benefit from some structure. Participation is more likely to be equal and the number of ideas generated usually will increase.

Some other hints for facilitating brainstorming groups:

1. Don't try to be one of the other group members. Save your ideas for when the group needs some prompting.
2. Be comfortable with short periods of silence. Silence often means that people are thinking—not that they have run out of ideas.
3. When idea productivity slows down, set a realistic quota of ideas to achieve (e.g., "try to think of five more ideas"). Or set a time limit.
4. Encourage humor and playfulness. Lead by example.

Other facilitation hints are provided in Chapter 13.

SIL method. This method relies upon forced relationships to generate ideas. In this regard, it is similar to many other idea-generation methods. The major difference is that the SIL method forces together ideas, while other methods force together problem elements or unrelated stimuli.

Consciously forcing together concepts can be difficult for some people. It requires a certain amount of practice. To demonstrate the process involved, you might select some sample problems and ask the most proficient group members to explain their thinking. Have them describe what they visualized or thought of to produce a combination. Once others learn this "secret," forced relationships are no longer so elusive.

Gordon/Little technique. Success with this method is largely dependent upon presentation of a problem in varying degrees of abstraction. To do this, you need to figure out what the "essence" is of what you need to accomplish. Does it involve preventing, reducing, increasing, changing, or modifying? Most problems can be described in one of these or other general ways. Then, you need to describe the same problem at a less abstract level. What is less abstract will be a subjective decision. However, you will need to think of at least two levels of abstraction for the technique to work effectively (ideally, you should try for three levels of abstraction).

Picture stimulation. I would agree with Geschka et al. (1981) that about 10 to 15 percent of the people who use this approach are dissatisfied with it and unsuccessful in thinking of new ideas. You should encourage these individuals to generate ideas on their own, while others use the method. This alternative is more productive than having a few people disrupt the session by criticizing the method or engaging in some unrelated activity.

When a group first describes a picture, encourage them to diverge as much as they can. Have them write down everything they see (or think they see). Above all, don't let them argue about what does and does not exist in a picture. Correctness of descriptions is not important, since the pictures are used only for their general stimulation value.

It is more important that the group focus upon action descriptions. Push them to write down more than just physical descriptions. Encourage them to look for movement and relationships between objects, major principles, and concepts. For instance, in a picture of a waterfall, the group needs to describe more than just water, rocks, and sky. Have them think about the force of the water and how it erodes rocks, is continually falling, and swirls around at the bottom. The more action oriented the descriptions are, the more likely it is that high quality ideas will result.

Greeting cards. A leader facilitating this method should ensure that a group doesn't become too playful. They need to maintain a task focus to generate ideas productively. You also may need to monitor the exchanges of cards between groups. Have the groups first use their own cards for stimulation. Then, they should exchange their cards with another group. If a group seems hesitant to use this method, you might suggest the variation involving individual cards.

Super heroes. Too much playfulness also can be a problem with this technique. However, allow plenty of time and don't be overly task oriented. When group members suggest ideas, focus upon one hero at a time. Have each person describe the powers of his or her character and any ideas stimulated. Then, encourage the other members to think of ideas based upon the hero.

Pin cards. Two difficulties commonly arise in using this method. The most common problem is people talking during the idea-writing phase. A gentle reminder that talking isn't permitted usually takes care of this problem. However, don't become overbearing and crack down on every whispered comment. Another difficulty involves bottlenecks that sometimes occur. Some group members are slower than others at passing the cards. As a result, cards pile up at one location. If this occurs, another gentle reminder to keep the cards moving should help.

Brainwriting pool. Like the pin cards method, this technique requires little leader facilitation. However, a leader or the group members themselves should ensure that no discussion occurs during idea generation. The only other major problem is likely to be a limited number of exchanges with the "pool." The fewer the exchanges, the less stimulation there will be. To remedy this problem, slower members should be encouraged to make more exchanges. There also should be no fewer than five people in each group (the more people, the more exchanges possible).

Method 6–3–5. A primary benefit of this technique is its structured approach to idea generation. However, you also should encourage some flexibility of application. You don't "have" to use six people, three ideas, or five minutes. The technique could be modified. As method 5–10–5, for example, five people would generate ten ideas for five minutes. Changing the numbers still retains the structure and allows for some experimentation.

Collective notebook. A major problem of the CNB approach is maintaining a high participant motivation level. As a result, the participants should be selected for their interest in the problem, their willingness to participate, and their tendency to follow through on a task. The coordinator also can help by sending encouraging messages during the idea generation period and showing an overall interest in their idea-generation progress. Exchanging notebooks also should help motivation.

SUMMARY

Group idea-finding methods can be classified as either brainstorming or brainwriting variations. Brainstorming methods involve oral idea generation and include both structured and unstructured approaches. Structured brainstorming uses a set of agreed upon rules, while unstructured brainstorming involves no formal rules. Brainwriting approaches are either nominal (no face-to-face idea generation) or interacting (face-to-face idea generation).

Brainstorming advantages include accommodation of social interaction needs and potential for a high level of group cohesion. Brainstorming disadvantages include disruptive interpersonal conflicts and unequal participation. Brainwriting methods reduce or eliminate many brainstorming disadvantages and help ensure task orientation. However, brainwriting methods do not satisfy social interaction needs as well as brainstorming techniques. In general, both brainstorming and brainwriting approaches should be used whenever possible.

Divergence and convergence during idea-finding are similar for both individuals and groups. Divergence involves using a variety of methods to help spark ideas; convergence involves identifying hits, relates, and hotspots. After making any appropriate combinations and modifications, the selected ideas are evaluated further during solution-finding.

11
Solution-Finding

During idea-finding you should have "found" the raw material that forms solutions. Although some of your ideas may be well developed, most probably are solutions in the rough. You now are faced with the task of deciding which ideas have the potential for resolving your problem and which need additional work.

Making this decision involves more than applying critical, negative judgment. Your emphasis instead should be upon affirmative judgment. That is, you should look for the best features of your ideas and transform them into workable solutions. Instead of trying to reject ideas, you should use them to stimulate solutions.

OVERVIEW

Divergence during solution-finding consists of two activities. The first involves generating criteria for screening, selecting, and supporting ideas (Figure 11–1). These criteria help reduce and refine the total pool of ideas. They also are used to develop ideas into more workable solutions. The second divergent activity involves generating many solutions.

Convergence during this stage also involves two primary sets of activities (Figure 11–1). All of these activities are identical in process, but differ in the material used (i.e., criteria versus solutions). You first converge to screen, select, and support (strengthen) your evaluation criteria. Then, using these criteria, you converge to screen, select, and support problem solutions.

There is at least one side benefit of solution-finding that often is overlooked. Examining criteria and transforming ideas into solutions helps lay

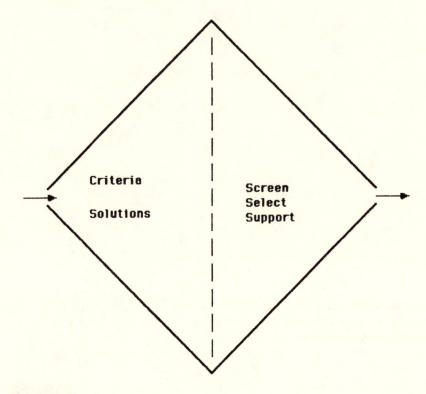

Figure 11–1
Solution-Finding

the groundwork for your plan of action. Solution-finding activities provide a natural bridge to acceptance-finding.

DIVERGING AND CONVERGING

In contrast to the other stages, there are two divergent and convergent processes during solution-finding. Since these processes are interrelated during solution-finding, they will be discussed together.

You should begin divergence by generating a list of potential criteria to use in evaluating your ideas. As with any divergent activity, you should defer all judgment. Try to generate as many criteria as possible without regard to their apparent usefulness.

Understanding and using criteria. Criteria are standards you use to assess ideas. They are the decision elements that must be satisfied to guide a choice. For instance, we use outside temperature to determine what clothes to wear.

When we make choices in everyday life, we use criteria to some extent. Usually, these criteria are implicit. We may not even be aware that we are using them. For example, even a simple act such as deciding what to eat in a restaurant involves criteria. You might consider such factors as how hungry you are, cost of different items, and time required to cook a particular food. However, when we select a food, we may not be fully aware of why we have chosen it. Often, we experience the most trouble in decision making when we are unaware of the criteria we are using.

In many situations, decision making is easier when the criteria are more explicit. However, your criteria won't be explicit unless you consciously search them out. That's why it is important to think of as many criteria as you can. Then, you can use them to guide your decision making and formation of solution alternatives.

Many criteria will apply only to certain types of problems; other criteria are more universal and will apply more broadly. For example, such factors as time, cost, usefulness, acceptability, and likelihood of success will be broadly applicable. Others, in contrast, must be generated specifically for a particular problem.

When you generate criteria, try to be as specific as possible. Instead of saying "low cost," for example, specify something like "costs less than $100." You also should try to specify the direction of "neutral" criteria whenever you use a general criterion. Thus, if you use cost as a criterion and don't specify an amount, you at least should list it as "low" cost.

During solution-finding, criteria can be used in three different ways: screening, selecting, and supporting (Isaksen & Treffinger, 1985). Screening helps to reduce a large pool of ideas to a more manageable number. It also helps to refine ideas. Selecting is an intermediate step for choosing the best of the remaining ideas. And supporting is used to modify or transform ideas into workable solutions.

Screening. When you finished convergence during idea-finding, you should have selected a number of ideas for further consideration. You should have at least three or four ideas and possibly more, depending upon how selective you were. If you only have a few ideas, you probably won't need to do much screening. However, if you have more than three or four ideas, you may want to reduce the total to make them easier to analyze.

One simple way to reduce a number of ideas is to select one or two important criteria. Next, compare each idea with each criterion and eliminate those ideas that do not satisfy the criterion. The remaining ideas then can be evaluated more intensively. However, be careful when using this approach, since a potentially useful idea can be eliminated on the basis of a single criterion.

Consider the following list of ideas for dealing with a typical problem in the airline industry: IWWM we increase customer satisfaction on international flights?

1. Minimize delays in take-offs.
2. Inject scented air into air vents.
3. Provide adjustable temperature air vents for each passenger.
4. Install moveable seats that swivel and recline.
5. Make the seat temperature adjustable.
6. Install lumbar support controls in seats.
7. Install a vibrating unit in each seat.
8. Set up an exercise area.
9. Install portable, "for rent" computers in seatbacks.
10. Increase the size of restrooms.
11. Provide free popcorn during movies.
12. Offer business and personal development seminars (at cost).

Two criteria for screening these ideas might be cost and potential for attracting new customers. First, I select all those ideas that cost below a certain amount (revenue losses incurred from using an idea also should be considered). Thus, I might select ideas 2, 3, 5, 7, 9, 11, and 12. I then rate each of these ideas for their potential to attract new customers. In doing this, I give the highest rating to ideas 7, 9, and 12. However, rather than eliminate the other ideas (i.e., ideas 2, 3, 5, and 11), I might keep those that satisfy my cost criterion. Or, I might apply a more stringent cost criterion to further reduce the list. As a result, my final list might include ideas 2, 7, 9, 11, and 12.

Ideas initially eliminated using the first criterion don't always be need to be added after evaluation with the second criterion. You should remain flexible, open to new information about your criteria.

Selecting. Selecting is an additional way to reduce and refine the remaining ideas. It is more systematic than screening and provides a more in-depth analysis of ideas. For many problems, selecting will be the last solution-finding activity.

Selecting is easier using a weighted decision matrix. Such a matrix uses both divergence and convergence to guide you in choosing the one or two best ideas. In contrast to screening, selection criteria are weighted in terms of their relative importance (unless all evaluation criteria are of equal importance).

The basic steps for setting up a decision matrix are:

1. Generate a list of all possible selection criteria.
2. Select the best criteria (usually at least five).
3. Using a 1- to 5-point scale, assign a weight to each criterion in terms of how important it is to you (5 = very important; 1 = relatively unimportant).

4. Using a 1- to 5-point scale, rate each idea on each criterion (5 = excellent, 4 = very good, 3 = satisfactory, 2 = needs improvement, 1 = unacceptable).

5. Multiply each criterion importance weighting by each idea rating to obtain a subtotal for each idea.

6. Add up the products from step 5 and evaluate the results for further action.

An illustration of a weighted decision matrix is shown in Figure 11–2. Using the previous example involving airline customer satisfaction, criteria are generated as shown. Next, the criteria are weighted in importance and each idea is rated on each criterion. For example, the criterion involving a positive return on investment is given a weight of 5. The ideas then are rated on this criterion (positive ROI). In this case, scented air is rated as 1, vibrating seats is given a 2, computers a 5, popcorn a 1, and seminars a 5. Next, these ideas are rated on the remaining criteria and the subtotals are calculated for each. Finally, the subtotals are summed. In this example, seminars is the highest rated idea, followed by computers, vibrating seats, popcorn, and scented air.

Depending upon organizational priorities, all or none of these ideas may be implemented. And, the order in which they are implemented may vary. Receiving a high rating is no guarantee that an idea will or should be implemented first. The purpose of the decision matrix is to serve as an aid in decision making. It can help structure what often is a very unstructured and unsystematic process.

The ratings obviously are subjective and not intended to provide the definitive answer to the airline's problems. However, such a matrix has an advantage over strictly intuitive decision making. With a matrix, you can evaluate more factors than the human mind can process at one time. As a result, the final decision is more likely to be higher in quality and reflect the "true" feelings of the decision maker.

If you are dissatisfied or uncomfortable with the outcome of a decision matrix, reevaluate the selection process. You may discover that you left out some important criteria. Or, you may have rated some factors according to how you thought you should rather than how you actually felt. In either case, a reevaluation sometimes can produce more satisfying results.

Supporting. An often overlooked function of criteria involves using them to diverge and generate solutions. This function is consistent with the principle of affirmative judgment. If you rate an idea low on some criteria, you frequently can improve the rating (and the ideas) by making some alterations. Using the criteria as a guide, you may be able to improve ideas. Or, you may be able to think of other ways to modify or even combine ideas. Your goal is to develop a workable solution.

Contrary to the approach many people use, decision making should not be a negative process in which you try to eliminate as many alternatives as

	Importance	Scented air	Subtotal	Vibrating seats	Subtotal	Computers	Subtotal	Popcorn	Subtotal	Seminars	Subtotal
Positive ROI	5	1	5	2	10	5	25	1	5	5	25
Attract new customers	5	1	5	3	15	5	25	1	5	3	15
Implement in three months	3	5	15	2	6	2	6	5	15	4	12
Meets safety standards	5	5	25	4	20	5	25	5	25	5	25
Few structural changes	5	5	25	5	25	4	20	5	25	5	25
Acceptable to customers	5	3	15	4	20	3	15	3	15	3	15
No new duties for personnel	4	5	20	4	16	4	16	2	8	4	16
Minimal maintenance	4	3	12	5	20	4	16	4	16	5	20
Minimal training	3	5	15	4	12	4	12	5	15	4	12
No new equipment	2	3	6	1	2	1	2	2	4	5	10
TOTALS:			143		136		162		133		175

Figure 11–2
Weighted Decision Matrix

possible through negative criticism. Instead, decision making might be better viewed as an opportunity to practice and use a positive approach to solution development.

In the selection illustration shown in Figure 11–2, several improvements using idea combinations are possible. As one example, computers and seminars might be combined to suggest such new ideas as: seminars on how to use computers, computer-assisted instruction to teach or assist learning of a particular topic, and persuading instructors to teach seminars by offering them free computers.

Not all improvements need to result from combinations, however. Some improvements can be made to single ideas. For example, the idea of vibrating seats might be improved upon by elaborating upon different aspects of the idea. Thus, vibration might be limited to the seatback, the seat, or both. And operation of the seats might be controlled by a coin box to make the seats financially "self-supporting" (if you'll excuse the pun).

Ideas don't always need to be improved or combined with others to produce better solutions. One or more ideas you have selected from a matrix analysis might stand alone as solutions. As a result, you won't have to do much supporting. If an idea can be implemented as is and if it appears to have the potential to resolve your problem, go ahead and use it as a solution.

If you work in a group, the odds might increase that an idea can be improved or combined. With the appropriate climate and group skills, a group's combined resources can make it easier to transform ideas. Through stimulation of others, you might think of several improvements that would elude you as an individual.

You will have finished solution-finding when you are satisfied that you have at least one solution that can resolve your problem. However, you also should consider selecting a "backup" solution. Implementation obstacles often arise that you failed to consider or they don't become known until new information is available. These obstacles will be dealt with during acceptance-finding.

GUIDELINES FOR TRAINERS

Two major points should be emphasized during solution-finding. Just mentioning these points usually is not enough. Class members also need to experience and discuss them.

The first point concerns the importance of affirmative judgment. Our conditioning has taught us to make decisions using negative criticism. However, it can be more productive to also consider the positive value of ideas before rejecting them. Thus, have your class practice improving or combining ideas even if the ideas appear workable at the outset. Sometimes deliberate analysis and toying around with ideas can suggest new approaches.

The second point involves cautioning the class about overreliance upon decision matrices. Matrices are intended only to provide some structure to the decision-making process; they are a means to an end and not an end by themselves. It often is tempting to interpret quantitative totals as indicators of the final selections. In some cases this may work out. However, most decision situations can't be resolved so neatly. Further analysis usually is required. In particular, criteria often need to be modified, added, or deleted. Moreover, the ratings themselves sometimes need to be revised.

Another point to emphasize concerns using groups to do a decision matrix. Time often is limited or conflict exists among the group members. As a result, the members may have to struggle to achieve any degree of consensus. Frequently, they make little progress and become extremely dissatisfied with the process.

To overcome this situation, it sometimes helps to suggest using voting and averaging. If it is available, some time should be used for discussion. Next, group members should rate each idea (individually) on each criterion. Finally, the ratings can be averaged to determine the outcome. Although such an approach is not ideal, it can simplify the process and cause the group to become more task oriented.

SUMMARY

Unlike the other stages, solution-finding consists of two sets of divergent and convergent activities. The first divergent activity involves generating all the potential criteria you can think of. Next, converge and select the best criteria. Then, using these criteria as judgment standards, converge and select the best ideas. Finally, you should diverge using your chosen ideas and try to develop the best solution possible.

There are at least two major advantages to using criteria during solution-finding. First, your decision making will be more explicit than implicit. As a result, the final selection should be higher in quality. Second, if you assign different degrees of importance to each criterion, your decision making will more accurately reflect your perceptions. That is, weighted criteria allow you to acknowledge that not all criteria are equal in importance.

Three primary processes used during solution-finding are: screening, selecting, and supporting. Screening involves selecting one or two important criteria and using them to reduce a large number of ideas. For instance, you might eliminate all ideas that would cost more than $1,000 to implement. Selecting is a more systematic process for choosing ideas than screening. Weighted criteria are placed in a matrix with chosen ideas and rated to select the one or two "best" ideas. Finally, supporting involves using the principle of "affirmative judgment" to improve any previously considered ideas. Ways are considered to improve an idea or two or more ideas are combined to produce a better solution.

If you use quantitative ratings to help screen, select, or support ideas, interpret the results with caution. Such ratings are subjective and the outcome will not always be satisfactory. If you are dissatisfied with your ratings, review the criteria and the scores you gave to the criteria and the ideas. It could be that you will want to add some criteria or revise your ratings.

Trainers should emphasize the importance of affirmative judgment during solution-finding. The negative aspects of eliminating solution alternatives from contention should be downplayed. Instead, all ideas should be evaluated for their potential to stimulate new or modified solutions. Another point to emphasize is that it can be difficult to achieve consensus if groups are used during solution-finding. To overcome this problem, group members can individually rate ideas and the results then can be averaged. However, consensus should be attempted first.

12
Acceptance-Finding

Once you have finished solution-finding, you may be ready to begin acceptance-finding. If you have selected a high-quality solution and anticipate few major obstacles, you can develop a plan of action and implement your solution. Then, you can sit back and watch your problem be resolved. Or can you?

After selecting a solution, a natural tendency is to implement it as soon as possible. However, such an action may be hasty. Your eagerness to resolve a problem could make things worse. Or, at the very least, the problem could continue unaffected.

Before implementing any solution, you should be confident in its ability to resolve your problem. Otherwise, you may have wasted your efforts. Should you consider bypassing acceptance-finding, weigh your decision against three criteria: time available, problem importance, and strength of implementation obstacles.

Obviously, if your problem must be resolved immediately, you won't be able to devise a carefully thought out plan of action. You will have to make do with the time available. How important you perceive your problem to be also may help with your decision. If you don't have much to lose from an unsuccessful solution, then acceptance-finding may not be critical. If the time is available, you always can try again. The third decision criterion is strength of implementation obstacles. The more likely it is that an obstacle will prevent implementation, the more important it will be to use acceptance-finding.

IMPORTANCE OF ACCEPTANCE-FINDING

The importance of this stage stems from the need to "sell" yourself on your solution. That is, you must accept your solution before you can expect anyone else to. Also, if you have any uncertainty about the potential value of a solution, acceptance-finding can help reduce or eliminate this uncertainty.

In addition to gaining acceptance from yourself, acceptance-finding helps gain acceptance from others. In contrast to the previous stages where the focus was upon what was acceptable to you, this stage also forces you to consider what will be acceptable to others. Because it can be more action oriented than the other stages, acceptance-finding usually requires more person-to-person interaction. Others frequently must be consulted before you can implement a solution.

A typical instance involving acceptance of others is when you must "sell" your solution to your boss or someone else in an authority position. However, the reverse situation also occurs. A manager frequently needs to sell other employees (subordinates and otherwise) on an idea.

A third reason for the importance of acceptance-finding is that it forces you to develop and evaluate all obstacles that might hinder implementation. Some solutions are more difficult to implement than others. Depending upon the prevailing climate in your organization and a variety of other factors, you may find yourself stuck with a wonderful solution, but no way to implement it. However, if you systematically evaluate obstacles and devise ways to overcome them, you will increase the odds for successful implementation.

A fourth reason for the importance of acceptance-finding is its role in neutralizing "Murphy's Law" and its various corollaries. As you may know, Murphy's Law states: "If anything can go wrong, it will." Some corollaries of this law are:

- Nothing is as easy as it looks.
- When you identify three things that could go wrong and develop ways to circumvent them, a fourth will promptly develop.
- Everthing takes longer than you think.
- Nothing is foolproof because fools are so ingenious.

Of course, you can't expect to circumvent Murphy's Law completely. However, by making a deliberate attempt to deal with it, you can reduce many of its effects.

OVERVIEW

You should begin acceptance-finding by diverging and generating a list of "assisters and resisters" (Isaksen & Treffinger, 1985). These are factors that can help or hinder solution implementation. Next, converge and select the most important assisters and resisters. If little time is available, you could use the assisters and resisters to develop an action plan. However, if you can do a more thorough analysis, a second activity would be a potential problem analysis (PPA) (Kepner & Tregoe, 1965; 1981). This technique will help you systematically identify, evaluate, and overcome major implementation obstacles.

After planning to overcome obstacles, you should develop a specific plan of action. This plan should detail who will do what, where, when, and how. An implementation checklist and criteria from solution-finding can be used to develop this plan. In addition, your plan should consider the issues of ownership, motivation to implement, and ability to influence the plan.

As shown in Figure 12–1, the assisters and resisters, the potential problem analysis, and the plan of action all bridge both divergent and convergent phases of acceptance-finding. However, there are activities that are primarily convergent. These activities are: screening, selecting, supporting, and recycling. Screening and selecting occur whenever you try to reduce the number of assisters and resisters, general implementation obstacles, or action plan alternatives. The supporting activity is used to help strengthen your PPA or plan of action. Finally, recycling is used to monitor the progress of your solution and make any necessary adjustments. In some situations, you even may want to return to a previous stage in the model.

DIVERGING AND CONVERGING

Assisters and resisters. The first acceptance-finding activity involves generating a list of assisters and resisters (Isaksen & Treffinger, 1985). Assisters are all those factors that can help gain acceptance for your solution; resisters are all those factors that can hinder solution acceptance. To structure the information-gathering process involved, you might try the five W's and H method that you used during fact-finding. In this case, you would look for the people (who?), things (what?), locations (where?), times (when?), reasons (why?), and steps (how?) associated with various assisters and resisters.

To illustrate this process, I will use the solution chosen for the problem of increasing international airline passenger satisfaction (Chapter 11). In this case, the highest-rated solution was to provide business and personal development seminars during international flights.

Potential solution assisters are:

People: Airline pilots and cabin personnel; companies and consultants who conduct seminars; passengers interested in such seminars.

Things: The upper deck of a 747 airplane; earphones and connections already in place; a video machine and screen; and, the fold-down tray tables for writing.

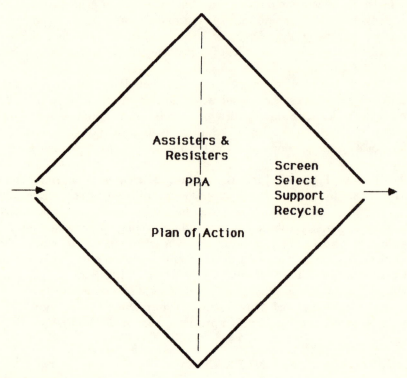

Figure 12–1
Acceptance-Finding

Locations: Popular foreign cities and resorts as attractions to participate.

Times: Seminars during the early portions of overseas flights would help pass the time.

Reasons: Attending seminars while flying would combine two activities and use time more efficiently; some portion of traveling expenses might be tax deductible, and, if participants remained on the upper deck, more seats would be available below.

Steps: Conduct a marketing survey to test passenger reaction.

Potential solution resisters are:

People: First class passengers who resent the upper deck being used for the seminars; seminar companies who might resent the competition; and seminar instructors who are not invited to participate.

Things: Inflexible seating arrangements could hinder small group discussions; noise might make it difficult to hear.

Locations: Flights to undesirable locations might make it difficult to obtain the best instructors; the upperdeck can accommodate only a limited number of participants.

Times: Jet lag might retard learning retention; conducting the seminars during the later portions of flights probably wouldn't be effective.

Reasons: People will be more interested in relaxing during a long flight; one boring instructor could jeopardize the entire program.

Steps: Make the seminars too long; forget to include experiential exercises.

When generating assisters and resisters it is important that you really push to identify as many factors as you can. Overlooking one element at this point in the process could make the difference between success and failure. You also should not worry if there is some overlap among the categories. The appropriateness of information within the categories is relative. Whether something belongs under the "times" or "reasons" categories, for example, is not important. Nor is it critical whether something is categorized as an assister or resister. It is important, however, that you generate as much data as possible.

Identifying "hits" and "relates." Once you have developed a list of assisters and resisters, you should identify "hits" and "relates." That is, note what you consider to be important and look for commonalities among the data. For instance, in the previous example the hits (in italics) might be identified as follows:

Assisters:

People: Airline pilots and *cabin personnel*, companies and *consultants* who conduct seminars, passengers who would be interested in such seminars.

Things: The *upper deck* of a 747 airplane, *earphones and connections already in place*, a *video machine and screen*, and the fold-down tray tables for writing.

Locations: *Popular foreign cities and resorts* as attractions to participate.

Times: Seminars during the *early portions of overseas flights* would help pass the time.

Reasons: Attending seminars while flying would *combine two activities* and use time more efficiently, some portion of traveling expenses might be *tax deductible*, and, if participants remained on the upperdeck, *more seats would be available* below.

Steps: *Conduct a marketing survey* to test passenger reaction.

Resisters:

People: *First class passengers who resent the upper deck being used* for the seminars, seminar companies who might resent the competition, and seminar instructors who are not invited to participate.

Things: *Inflexible seating arrangements* could hinder small group discussions; *noise* might make it difficult to hear.

Locations: Flights to *undesirable locations* might make it difficult to obtain the best instructors; the upper deck can accommodate only a *limited number of participants*.

Times: Jet lag might retard learning retention; conducting the seminars during the later portions of flights probably wouldn't be effective.

Reasons: People will be more interested in relaxing during a long flight; one *boring instructor* could jeopardize the entire program.

Steps: Make the seminars *too long*, forget to include *experiential exercises*.

I then might group the hits into five clusters:

People: Cabin personnel, consultants, first class passengers, type and number of participants.

Seminars: Length, format (lecture, discussion, experiential), topics.

Physical Environment: Seating arrangements, number of seats available, seminar equipment availability, noise, the upper deck.

Attitudes: Resentment by first class passengers, satisfaction with seminars and social interactions, feeling of being tired, general fun of participation, frustration with boring material or instructors.

Financial Benefits: Tax deductible to many participants, more seats will be available to generate income, seminars might attract more passengers, free travel for consultants.

After looking over all the hits and developing these categories, several areas might emerge as important. These probably should be considered prior to implementation. Developing the categories also might help you think of other concerns to include in an action plan. For example, the social interaction that accompanies group exercises might be an additional assister.

The next step is to use the information generated so far to guide development of an action plan. If there is little time available or you don't want to expend much effort, this plan would be your next-to-last acceptance-finding step. The final activity is to implement your solution, monitor its progress, and recycle to any previous stages if required. However, to do a more thorough acceptance-finding analysis, the next step would be to do a potential problem analysis (PPA).

Potential Problem Analysis. The PPA procedure originally was developed by Kepner and Tregoe (1965; 1981) and later modified by Woods and Davies (1973). The version presented here was developed by VanGundy (1984) and represents only minor variations from those that preceded it.

The steps for a PPA are:

1. Diverge and generate as many potential problems as you can think of.
2. Using a seven-point scale, rate the probability of occurrence (P) and the seriousness (S) of each problem (1 = low probability/seriousness; 7 = high probability/seriousness).

3. Multiply each probability rating by each seriousness rating and write down the results (PS).

4. Think of at least one preventive action for each problem.

5. Using a seven-point scale, estimate the probability that a problem will exist after the preventive actions are taken. This result is known as the residual probability (RP).

6. Multiply each PS score times each RP score and record the results for each problem listed (PS × RP).

7. Develop contingency (backup) plans for each problem receiving a high PS × RP score. If time is available and you consider the problem to be important, develop contingency plans for all the problems.

An illustration of this procedure is shown in Figure 12–2. Using the solution of in-flight seminars, four potential problems are shown. The probability of each is rated along with its seriousness to obtain the PS score. Preventive actions then are developed for each problem. For example, conducting a marketing survey is suggested as a way to circumvent low passenger interest. Results of the survey could be used to tailor the seminars to areas of passenger interest. Residual probabilities (RP) are estimated next, followed by the product of the PS score times the RP score. Finally, contingency or backup plans are developed for each potential problem analyzed. (In this case, contingency plans for the problem of boring material might have been omitted due to the relatively low PS × RP score.)

The above example is simplified considerably. More problems and detail should be added to analyze the potential problems adequately. Moreover, a number of additional preventive actions and contingency plans should be developed. On the other hand, the quantitative ratings could be used as presented. However, be careful about placing too much emphasis upon subjective evaluations.

DEVELOPING AN ACTION PLAN

The next acceptance-finding activity is to develop a plan of action. This plan should carefully detail who will do what, where, when, how, and why. It should function as a map of how you can implement your solution. When combined with a PPA, your action plan should help ensure implementation success.

An action plan should consider three levels of activity: immediate, short range, and long range. Immediate activities are things you can accomplish within a day or so; short-range activities are those you plan to do in the near future (e.g., a few weeks or months); long-range actions are those that might be implemented within a year or so, depending upon the nature of the problem and the general implementation environment (some environments may be more conducive to a particular solution than others). Of

PROBLEMS	P	S	PS	PREVENTIVE ACTIONS	RP	PSxRP	CONTINGENCY PLANS
1. First class passengers resent loss of upper deck	7	6	42	Free seminar attendance; note deck only used a short time.	3	126	Give airline ticket discounts; provide special enter- tainment in First Class
2. Low passenger interest	5	7	35	Conduct survey	3	105	Use entertaining instructors
3. Boring instructors	4	6	24	Obtain references	5	120	Screen instructors using preview sessions
4. Boring material	4	7	14	Preview material	2	28	Require experiential exercises

Figure 12–2
Potential Problem Analysis

these three action levels, long-range activities will be the most subject to change. Most actions at this level should be considered tentative.

There are at least five sources you can use to develop your plan: assisters and resisters, a PPA, an implementation checklist, solution-finding criteria for supporting the solution, and a check of ownership, motivation, and influence. Not all of these sources will be required to implement every solution. In fact, there are even more complex implementation procedures you might want to consider, such as PERT charts (e.g., Moder & Phillips, 1970). You will have to decide how much time you have and how much effort you want to expend.

Much of your action plan can be drawn from your analysis of the assisters and resisters. By examining each factor listed, you should think of many specific actions needed to ensure successful implementation.

The preventive actions and contingency plans you listed during your PPA also are excellent sources of material for guiding development of your plan. You probably can incorporate much of this data into your plan. Usually, you just need to decide upon the order in which you should accomplish each action.

Another useful source of data for action plans is an implementation checklist. Such a list usually is based upon the "five W's and H" method. You can examine a list of who, what, where, when, why, and how questions and see if any action steps are suggested. Such a list might contain the following types of questions:

- Who could help you implement your solution?
- From whom do you need to gain acceptance?
- Who has implemented a similar solution successfully?
- What is most likely to facilitate implementation?
- What are the major benefits of your solution?
- What resources do you need for implementation?
- What is the most important first step?
- What is the most important last step?
- What individuals and groups are most likely to support your solution?
- Where in the plan are you likely to encounter the most resistance?
- Where are you likely to encounter the most support?
- Where in the plan do you need to test all your assumptions?
- When should you take the first action?
- When is the best time to seek acceptance and support from others?
- When should you revise your plan?
- How is implementing this solution different from others?
- How will other people benefit from your solution?
- How should you approach others to gain their acceptance?
- How should you seek feedback about the solution's success?

In addition to these questions, there probably are many others that you could add. Or, you may want to modify some of these to best suit your needs. In any event, such a list often can prompt many questions you might have overlooked.

Speaking of overlooking things, you might have noticed that there are no "why" questions in the list. This was an intentional omission. Why questions should be used to build a rationale for all of the other questions. That is, after you answer each question, ask "Why?" of your answer. For example, if you state that your boss is most likely to support your solution, ask yourself why you believe that. By examining each answer in this manner, you automatically will test many assumptions that you might have overlooked otherwise. Any one of these assumptions could be the key to successful problem resolution.

A potential fourth source of data for an action plan is the evaluation criteria you generated during solution-finding. These criteria often can support your solution by strengthening its implementation. As an example, the solution-finding matrix in Chapter 11 included the criteria:

Positive ROI

Ability to attract new customers

Can be implemented within three months

Meets safety standards

Requires few structural changes

Acceptable to customers

Requires no new duties for cabin personnel

Requires minimal maintenance

Requires minimal training

Requires no new equipment

For the solution of in-flight seminars, some of these criteria might suggest elements of an action plan such as:

• Include detailed financial information for persuading higher management (positive ROI).

• Conduct a marketing survey that includes a market segment that has not flown your airline often. That is, what is it about the seminars that would be attractive to new customers?

• Make sure seating arrangements don't violate any emergency evacuation regulations (meets safety standards).

• Consult with cabin personnel representatives for their opinions (no new duties for personnel).

• Evaluate the physical condition and layout of all the potential upper deck areas that might be used (no new equipment).

These criteria also can help stimulate potential solution strengths and weaknesses when conducting a PPA or when listing assisters and resisters.

A final resource for developing an action plan is to evaluate the degree of solution ownership, motivation, and influence. If you have not already considered it, you will need to decide upon the actions for which you have responsibility. If you don't have ownership of an action, you will need to find out who does. Next, you should assess your overall motivation level. Depending upon how complex your solution is and the actions needed to implement it, you may be required to invest considerable time, money, and energy. In other words, you must decide how badly you want to solve your problem. If you are deficient in some resource, then you will want to plan how to acquire it. Finally, you should determine the amount of influence you can exert. Even if you have responsibility for an action, you may not be able to influence its implementation. Formal authority and informal influence often do not go hand in hand. The organization may have bestowed authority in the position you hold, but you may not have the personal influence required to get something done.

The last acceptance-finding activity involves implementing your solution and monitoring its progress. Whenever a deviation occurs, you should make needed adjustments. The solution-finding criteria and other data you generated during acceptance-finding sometimes can be used to make these adjustments.

You also may need to recycle your efforts, regardless of whether the problem is resolved. If the problem is resolved, you may want to recycle to objective-finding. A new challenge or opportunity might have arisen independent of the problem you have been working on. Or a new problem may have been created as a result of dealing with your original problem. If the problem is not resolved, you may need to recycle to another stage in the model to revise your approach for dealing with the problem. For instance, your perception of the original problem may have changed because of new information that became available. As a result, you may want to recycle to fact-finding or problem-finding.

GUIDELINES FOR TRAINERS

A natural tendency of many people is to gloss over acceptance-finding. At this point in the CPS process, you already have invested considerable time and effort. Impatience begins to set in and you are eager to try out your solution. However, such eagerness can be costly in the long run.

As a trainer, you should caution that acceptance-finding is an extremely important stage. In fact, some people argue that it is the most important stage. The best solutions won't help if they are not implemented properly. The problem solving "journey" is not complete at the end of solution-finding; it is just beginning.

Another point to stress is that acceptance-finding involves more than gaining acceptance from others. Individuals also must be willing to accept their own ideas. Otherwise, the commitment needed for implementation will be lacking. The same also holds true for groups.

A good way to illustrate the importance of acceptance-finding is to conduct an exercise. Have the class practice developing assisters and resisters in regard to some solution. Then, suggest that they develop their own variations to Murphy's Law. The data generated from the assisters and resisters often suggest many humorous versions of how things can go wrong.

Your class also will need to practice developing a PPA. When discussing this procedure, note the difference between preventive actions and contingency plans. Both are concerned with overcoming some problem obstacle. However, contingency plans usually are more costly (in terms of personnel, money, time, etc.) to implement. That is why contingency plans are considered "backup" actions—use them whenever less costly actions have failed. Admittedly, not all contingency plans will be more costly. However, this distinction should be drawn whenever possible.

As a final acceptance-finding activity, have your class practice developing action plans. They can do this as individuals, pairs, or in small groups. When they finish, have them present their plans to the other group members for discussion. Before starting this discussion, however, establish one ground rule: Both positive and negative comments are required.

To enforce this ground rule, rotate positive and negative comments in sequence. For example, one person would make a positive comment, the next person a negative comment, the third person a positive comment, and so forth until all comments have been made. If someone doesn't have a comment to make when it is their turn, they simply should say "pass."

A final point about acceptance-finding is to avoid premature convergence. This sometimes occurs during initial analysis of the assisters and resisters. If this analysis is too intense or concentrates too much upon a few key points, a broader perspective can be lost. When this occurs, a plan of action often is developed (often implicitly) before all potential problems and supporting elements have been adequately explored. To prevent this, encourage the class to evaluate many possible alternatives and reserve the formal plan of action for the end of convergence.

SUMMARY

Before implementing any solution, consider the potential obstacles you might encounter. If you have the time, consider the problem to be important, and perceive the obstacles to be difficult to overcome, use the acceptance-finding stage.

Acceptance-finding is important for a variety of reasons. First, you can use it to "sell" yourself on your solution. We usually need to convince ourselves about a solution's worth before we can convince others. Second, acceptance-finding can help you sell others on the merits of your solutions. Third, it forces you to consider all possible implementation obstacles and devise ways to overcome them. Finally, acceptance-finding is important because of its ability to help overcome Murphy's Law: "If anything can go wrong, it will."

You should begin acceptance-finding by generating a list of solution assisters and resisters. These are factors that can help or hinder implementation of your solution. Next, select the most important assisters and resisters. If time is limited and your motivation is low, use the assisters and resisters as stimuli to develop a plan of action. However, if more time is available and you want to analyze the situation more, do a potential problem analysis (PPA).

A PPA involves generating all possible implementation problems, rating the probability of occurrence (P) and seriousness (S) of each, developing preventive actions, rating the residual probabilities for the occurrence of each problem following preventive action (RP), and multiplying the product of PS by the RP scores to determine where contingency plans should be developed. (The higher the score, the more important it is to develop a contingency plan.)

A plan of action should consist of immediate, short-range, and long-range activities. The specific actions can be developed by analyzing the assisters and resisters, the PPA, an implementation checklist, solution-finding criteria for supporting the solution, and an evaluation of ownership, motivation, and potential influence.

Trainers should emphasize the importance of acceptance-finding and not allow it to be taken lightly. Various exercises also can demonstrate the importance of this stage. For example, potential problem analysis can be used to illustrate the difference between preventive actions and contingency plans. Contingency plans generally are considered to be relatively high-cost, backup plans; preventive actions typically are less costly to implement. Practice in developing action plans also can be beneficial as long as comments from others are both positive and negative.

13
Facilitating and Troubleshooting CPS Groups

If you plan to use CPS in groups or teach others how to use it, you should have some basic facilitation skills. In this chapter, I will briefly discuss the design of CPS training programs (illustrated with some examples from the corporate world) and provide some hints on facilitating CPS groups. Finally, I will present a list of troubleshooting situations and possible solutions for each.

DESIGNING TRAINING PROGRAMS

This section is not intended to serve as a comprehensive guide to training programs. If you want such a guide, you should consult any of the number of publications available in this area. Instead, I will focus upon some basics involved in setting up and conducting CPS training sessions.

1. Consider hiring an external consultant for initial advisement. CPS consultants can provide valuable advice on the major elements of a training program as well as how to get it started.

2. Perhaps the most important factor in successful internal programs is the groundwork needed to ensure system-wide support. Higher management must perceive a need for such a program and know that people are interested in it. They also must have realistic expectations about the possible benefits of CPS training. Once upper-level support is obtained, you then need to secure support from other managers and employees. Again, the potential benefits should be stressed.

3. One way to "sell" internal CPS training programs is to provide information about successes in other companies. However, the best way to introduce such training probably is through trial programs. If possible, try

to negotiate an arrangement for limited training involving only one small segment of the workforce. If the results are positive, the program then can spread to other areas.

4. People usually are receptive to something familiar. Creating motivation for a CPS program often can be done by first introducing the most familiar aspects of CPS. In most cases, this means that elements of idea-finding and solution-finding might be experimented with at the outset to "whet their appetite." The divergent aspects of idea-finding usually are popular with small groups and can be perceived as a lot of fun. Thus, before you provide training in the entire model, you first might expose them to some "fun" idea-generation techniques. Solution-finding also can prove to be popular with people who tend to be more analytical and linear in their thinking. The weighting of criteria and rating of different alternatives to produce quantitative totals can be very appealing to such types.

5. Once you have consulted with an external resource and sold the program idea to relevant personnel, consider developing a cadre of internal group facilitators. Selection of the appropriate people is extremely important, since their skills can determine the long-range success of the program. In addition to basic "platform" skills, such individuals should be able to create climates conducive to creative thinking, be receptive to new ideas, tolerate ambiguity, have a sense of humor, be nonjudgmental, feel comfortable working with groups, and be skilled and knowledgeable about the CPS process. A little enthusiasm also won't hurt.

6. The actual design of your program can vary considerably, depending upon the time, money, and number of personnel available to assist. However, the training process should follow the CPS model and provide sufficient practice. The outline used in this book or others on the topic could be used as guides. To illustrate what two companies have done, I will briefly describe their internal CPS programs. Both companies are technically oriented with a high proportion of scientists and engineers.

One company in the Midwest has used a one-half day format to train its managers in creative thinking:

a. A leader/facilitator begins by playing music and noting that the concepts to be discussed are "fuzzy."

b. The group discusses what creativity means to them. The facilitator notes that creativity is involved in more than new product development. It also is basic to day-to-day problem solving of a more general nature.

c. Various creative thinking obstacles are discussed and exercises are used to illustrate different principles (e.g., the nine-dot exercise discussed in this book).

d. As a warm-up activity, the class brainstorms ideas for a "real" problem involving the organization.

e. The philosophy behind suspension of judgment during divergent thinking is discussed. The facilitator emphasizes that even the negative aspects of most ideas can be modified to produce something more positive.

f. The facilitator leads a discussion on characteristics of creative individuals. When working with managers, he asks the class to consider the relevance of their descriptions to the type of creative person they would like to manage.

g. The facilitator leads a discussion on characteristics of the creative manager and how these characteristics might affect the overall organizational climate. (This discussion can be used with both managers and nonmanagers.)

h. The facilitator asks the class to describe what a creative organization might look like.

i. Finally, the class watches a movie involving an orchestra that is preparing to play Ravel's Bolero. The movie then is discussed in terms of similarities between the orchestra and a creative organization.

Another organization, Instrumentation Laboratory (IL) in Lexington, Massachusetts, devised a somewhat more extensive training program. Stimulated by the efforts of one of its managers, John Czaban, IL designed a two-day, monthly program that follows the CPS model.

After an hour of general introductions and warmup exercises, one hour is devoted to objective-finding. A short break is taken and the next two hours focus upon fact-finding. Following lunch, problem-finding is discussed and then idea-finding is presented in two parts. The first day concludes by using checklists to practice idea-finding. The second day begins with more idea-finding, but with a specific focus upon forming new associations. The rest of the morning includes sessions on solution-finding, acceptance-finding, and putting together the entire CPS process. The afternoon begins with a session on "making 'snap' decisions creatively," followed by 30 minutes on meeting methods. The remainder of the day is consumed with two group exercises in which participants' problems are dealt with by a group using the CPS model.

A core team of about nine managers functions as facilitators after attending a five-day training session conducted by an outside consultant. The group meets on a regular basis to compare notes and refine their program. A wide cross section of IL employees has been trained in CPS and their reactions have been favorable.

An approach I have designed is called TAPS (techniques, attitudes, process, structure). Techniques are specific methods for enhancing the CPS stages. Examples of such techniques have been described throughout this book. The attitudes component of TAPS involves training in basic creative thinking principles and exercises, such as those discussed in Chapters 2, 3, and 4. These attitudes need to be examined at the individual, group, and organizational levels. Process refers to the basic CPS model as well as all activities involved in establishing and maintaining a training program. Finally, structure involves any structural changes that might be needed to improve the generation, flow, and dissemination of ideas within the organization. For instance, some organizations create temporary work units to facilitate processing of ideas and their eventual implementation. The actual installation of such a program involves various training sessions at different levels throughout the organization.

FACILITATING CPS GROUPS

Each chapter in this book included guidelines for trainers to use when presenting the material. Some of these guidelines can be used as aids for facilitating the CPS process within a particular stage. There also are some more general guidelines for facilitating CPS groups. I have developed these guidelines from my experiences in working with groups and from various sources in the literature. An excellent reference is *A Facilitating Style of Leadership* by Sid Parnes (1985a). The following are presented in no particular order:

1. Make sure you have the necessary equipment and supplies, that everything is in working order, and that there are backups available if required. For a typical session, you will need plenty of flip charts, masking tape, markers or jumbo crayons, index cards, pens or pencils, writing paper, and, perhaps, tape recorders. If you can afford it, you might want to obtain a relatively new product that has revolutionized recording group-generated data. This product is similar to a portable chalkboard, but is written on with special pens. Then, whenever you want to make a copy of what is on the board, you push some buttons and up to 99 reproductions can be made. This is a lot easier than using flip chart paper and a written record is provided automatically. The only drawback may be the cost—currently about $3,500.

2. Use adequate rooms. Such variables as adequate lighting, temperature, and general aesthetics often are overlooked. If more than one group is involved, separate the groups so that one group will not be distracted by another. Also make sure that small tables are available, each seating five to seven people.

3. Before beginning any training or workshop sessions, establish ground rules with the participants. These ground rules should include such basics as an understanding about the time and length of breaks, meals, and whether smoking should be permitted. (I usually try to set up a smokers only area. If you do this, be careful that you don't affect group composition negatively—e.g., placing bosses and subordinates together.) Other ground rules might be developed to agree upon who will facilitate different phases, who will follow up after the meeting, and who will be responsible for reporting the results to others. Finally, ground rules also should include some description and practice with the four rules of brainstorming. Even experienced groups should practice brainstorming as a warmup exercise.

4. Whenever possible, use practice problems suggested by the group members. There usually will be a greater sense of ownership and motivation

to resolve the problem. Always write down the problem (using the "IWWM" format) in a location visible to all group members.

5. During divergence, encourage the group to really "stretch" themselves. Try setting quotas or using time limits to increase the quantity of ideas.

6. When discussing new idea generation techniques, first present those based upon free association (e.g., traditional brainstorming). Then, introduce methods that stimulate ideas using parts of the problem (e.g., semantic intuition). Save for last those techniques that rely upon unrelated problem stimuli (e.g., analogies, focused-object).

7. Try to model appropriate CPS behavior. Maintain a positive attitude and avoid any negative comments. Don't try to become a member of a group (a few contributions will be O.K., but don't overdo it). Do try to keep the group moving forward and be as enthusiastic as possible (without appearing insincere).

8. Don't be overly concerned with periods of silence. Some incubation can be beneficial.

9. Keep track of any time constraints and remind the groups about how much time remains.

10. During solution-finding and acceptance-finding, keep the group moving along. Encourage them to finish and remind them that their final objective is development of an action plan.

11. During relatively long sessions, encourage participants to move around. Just getting up and walking a little often can help clarify thoughts.

12. Don't assume that people will behave based upon what they say. For instance, you might explain a technique and ask if everyone understands how to use it. Even if most heads nod affirmatively, complete understanding may not exist. To assess understanding, watch the group actually use the technique and provide feedback if needed.

13. Try to develop and sustain an informal group atmosphere. For "serious" creativity, formal attire should be discouraged. Moving around and even sitting on the floor should be encouraged.

14. Practice effective listening techniques. Use reflective listening and check to ensure your understanding of what was said.

15. During convergence, encourage groups to use consensus seeking rather than simple voting. However, if little time is available, voting should be allowed.

TROUBLESHOOTING PROBLEMS AND SOLUTIONS

A variety of different problems are likely to occur during any CPS session. How you handle these problems can affect the climate of the session and may determine, in part, how successfully the problem is resolved. In this section, I describe some common situations faced by facilitators for which there is not always a ready solution. I then provide my opinion on how to

deal with these situations. Some general troubleshooting problems and solutions are discussed first, followed by problems and solutions pertaining
to each of the CPS stages.

General troubleshooting.

1. *Problem*: A group member begins to argue or debate about a procedure
or process used.

Possible solutions: • Ask the other group members to react to what is
happening and attempt to provide clarification. • Ask the disruptive member to meet with you after the session so that you can provide more individual attention. Avoid engaging in an argument or debate.

2. *Problem*: A group becomes bogged down and loses sight of what it
should be doing within a particular stage.

Possible solutions: • Ask a series of "why" questions to reframe their perspective of the stage. • Ask for clarification of the expectations of the group
members.

3. *Problem*: One or more group members attempt to dominate the discussion; other members have little opportunity to participate.

Possible solutions: • Ask the group to stop working on the problem and
briefly discuss how well they have been working together. Reflect any
opinions expressed. • Use brainwriting techniques to avoid all verbal activity. • Take the dominating member(s) aside during a break and discuss
the situation. In doing this, the focus should be upon the situational aspects
of the problem and not their behavior. Your objective is to improve the
situation, not the people.

4. *Problem*: The recorder/notetaker distorts what has been said or writes
down only what he or she wants to.

Possible solutions: • Rotate recorders. • Use a tape recorder or a staff person
not associated with the group. • Discuss the problem privately with the
individual involved.

5. *Problem*: You observe relatively long periods of silence within a group
and very little activity.

Possible solutions: • Ask the group members how they are doing. • If they
are satisfied with their progress, leave them alone now. However, check
on them again soon. • If they are dissatisfied with their progress, encourage
them to move on. • Suggest that they try certain techniques to structure their
activities (e.g., the "five W's and H" method). • Tell them what you have observed and ask for their suggestions. • Take a break and start over.

Troubleshooting during objective-finding.

1. *Problem*: A group has trouble generating lists of opportunities, challenges, and concerns.

Possible solutions: • Suggest that they develop a wish list. • Use a stimulator checklist. Parnes (1985a) suggests using something like the following:

Friends	Better
Relatives	Difficulties
Work	Concerns
Church	Responsibilities
Transportation	Complications
Money	Habits
Career	Attitudes
School	Choices
Home	Waste
Neighbors	Performance

Have the group see if any of the words from either column suggests a possible objective area. Then, have them combine one word from the first column with one from the second and use the combination for stimulation. For instance, "career" and "complications" might suggest: "IWWM I become promoted?"

2. *Problem*: The group becomes bogged down in developing the "perfect" wording for the objective statement.

Possible solutions: • Suggest that they try to develop a statement as if they were going to send a very expensive telegram. Encourage them to be economical with their words. • Suggest that they use newspaper headlines to write their statements.

3. *Problem*: As different concerns are suggested, one or more group members discuss possible solutions. The number of objective areas is decreased and other group members become frustrated with the lack of progress.

Possible solutions: • Suggest that the solutions be viewed as data that can be added to the list of possible objective areas. For instance, someone might suggest departmental finances as a potential objective area. Then, someone else might note that a good way to handle financial problems is to use a particular accounting procedure. In this case, the facilitator might suggest using accounting systems as another potential objective area. • If the previous solution does not resolve the problem, keep encouraging the group to think of more objective areas. • Privately discuss the problem with the chief offender.

Troubleshooting during fact-finding.

1. *Problem*: Group members disagree as to what is "fact" and what is "opinion."

Possible solutions: • Note that what appear to be opinions to us may be viewed as facts by the person suggesting them. A group does not have to develop consensus on all the facts proposed. In "fact," acknowledgment of all contributions as facts may go a long way toward increasing group cohesiveness and improving the overall group climate. • Encourage group members to withhold all evaluation during divergence. If people do not feel they are being evaluated, they may be more willing to open up with their "facts."

2. *Problem*: The group is dissatisfied with the facts generated. Most facts generated seem to be mundane and fail to get at the heart of the problem situation.

Possible solutions: • Suggest that they use an object unrelated to the problem area for stimulation. For example: What does the shape of a telephone receiver suggest? What does a computer suggest? What do the functions of a car engine suggest? • Suggest that they use analogies to stimulate additional data. Have them think about similiar problems and use the similarities for stimulation.

3. *Problem*: Group members are uncertain about when to stop collecting facts and move on to problem-finding.

Possible solutions: • Ask the group how uncertain they feel about the problem and how much ambiguity they are experiencing. If they appear to have a moderate degree of problem understanding, it probably is time to move on. Too much understanding can be dysfunctional. • Determine if the group experienced any "aha's" while generating facts. Development of important, new insights may signal that they can stop gathering facts.

Troubleshooting during problem-finding.

1. *Problem*: Group members believe that they already know what the problem is and are reluctant to participate in problem-finding.

Possible solutions: • Encourage the group to "stretch" their thinking and generate as many redefinitions as they can. • Suggest that the group consider "what if?" thinking to play around with the problem. Ask them to consider: "What if you didn't really know what the problem was? What possible ways could you define problem situations in this area?" • If the group resists all your efforts, consider that they may be right. Do not get involved in an argument over whether they actually know what the problem is. Simply indicate that it may be safer to at least check out some other possibilities. Since little time is involved, what have they got to lose?

2. *Problem*: The group seems to be locked in on a narrow problem perspective. The wider aspects and implications of the problem situation are not being considered.

Possible solutions: • Use the "why method" (Chapter 8) to broaden the group's problem perspective. • Suggest that the group look at several problems they have identified and consider how each of these problems might be viewed as a cause of another problem. For instance, the problem "IWWM we reduce conflict within our team?" might be the focus of a group's efforts. If they view conflict as a cause, however, broader problems might be suggested. In this case, they might note how conflict hinders productivity and use the problem: "IWWM we increase our productivity?" Reducing conflict then could become a possible solution to be considered later on.

3. *Problem*: The group cannot seem to generate many different problem definitions.

Possible solutions: • Suggest that they substitute different verbs and verb phrases to suggest new perspectives. • Ask them to assume that they have five minutes to develop five more statements or they will be fired. (Make sure they know you are kidding if you are their boss!)

4. *Problem*: The group is having trouble deciding upon the best problem statement to select for idea-finding.

Possible solutions: • Tell the group that there may be no "best" problem definitions for their situation. However, since they have spent time exploring all aspects of the situation, potential ideas may emerge during idea-finding that they can use to crystallize their problem perceptions. Therefore, they should select the best definition for the situation and not worry about achieving perfection. • If all else fails, suggest using a weighted decision matrix (Chapter 11) or voting. However, caution the group to select the one statement that seems to best incorporate their concerns.

Troubleshooting during idea-finding.

1. *Problem*: The group slows down during idea divergence. They seem to be running out of ideas.

Possible solutions: • Encourage them to stretch their thinking. • Establish realistic idea quotas and deadlines. • Have the group members move around. • Try brainwriting approaches (Chapter 10). • Use idea checklists such as the Product Improvement CheckList (PICL™) (VanGundy, 1985). • Coach the group on how to build upon the ideas of others. • Take a break.

2. *Problem*: The quality of the ideas appears to be declining or nonexistent. Very few unique ideas are being proposed.

Possible solutions: • Use analogies (Chapter 9), picture stimulation, greeting cards (Chapter 10), or other methods that rely upon unrelated problem stimuli to generate ideas. • Encourage them to think of the silliest possible idea; then, have them modify it to be more practical. • Change the composition of the group: Bring in someone new or ask all group members to move temporarily to another group. • Try imagery and relaxation techniques. • Take a break.

3. *Problem*: One or more group members have trouble withholding evaluation of the ideas proposed.

Possible solutions: • Observe the group some more and see if the other members might be censoring the guilty parties. After explaining and discussing the brainstorming rules, groups often will monitor themselves. • If the group is not self-monitoring or if it is not effective, gently remind the group about the importance of deferring judgment. • Note that there will be plenty of time for evaluating ideas during idea-finding convergence and during solution-finding.

4. *Problem*: The group is uncertain as to when they should stop idea-finding and begin solution-finding.

Possible solutions: • Determine if the group has produced many insights into their problem. If they have, it may be time to move on. • Determine if the group has had several spurts of divergent activity—if the ideas seemed to come faster than they could be recorded. If they have, they may want to stop idea-finding. • Select a few of the most promising ideas and informally evaluate them against two or three important criteria. If the ideas do not satisfy the criteria to the group's (or client's) satisfaction, continue to look for more ideas.

Troubleshooting during solution-finding.

1. *Problem*: Group members have trouble generating evaluation criteria.

Possible solutions: • Use analogies. • Use the "five W's and H" technique. • Generate a list of one idea's advantages and disadvantages. Use this list to stimulate criteria for other ideas. • Develop lists of "musts" and "wants" and use them to stimulate criteria.

2. *Problem*: Some group members do not clearly understand the concept and importance of weighted criteria.

Possible solutions: • Have the group practice generating criteria using a familiar example, such as buying a new car. • Ask someone who currently is making a decision about something to describe the situation and the criteria involved.

3. *Problem*: Group members argue about criterion weights or how to rate different solutions.

Possible solutions: • If little time is available, suggest averaging individual scores. • Encourage the group to work toward consensus.

4. *Problem*: After converging, two or more solutions appear to be almost equal in potential to resolve the problem.

Possible solutions: • If feasible, implement all the solutions—either all at once or in an appropriate order. • Use one or more of the solutions to help deal with subproblems. • Flip a coin.

Troubleshooting during acceptance-finding.

1. *Problem*: Group members want to "jump the gun" and implement the chosen solution.

Possible solutions: • Remind them that they already have spent much effort developing the solution and should not jeopardize their success at this stage. • Note that examining acceptance-finding activities can reveal ways to improve the solution and increase the odds of successful implementation even more.

2. *Problem*: Group members begin to converge upon a plan of action before fully considering possible implementation obstacles.

Possible solutions: • Tell the group: "Don't do that!" • Failing that admonishment, have the group members individually generate lists of possible obstacles and ways to overcome them. Then, have them share their lists and develop a master group list.

3. *Problem*: Group members have difficulty generating enough potential implementation obstacles.

Possible solutions: • Use a general checklist of implementation stimulators. For example, Parnes (1985a) suggests such questions as:

What might I do to gain acceptance? How? When? Where? Why?

What additional resources might help? How might I obtain them?

How might I improve, safeguard, or fortify the idea?

Who might add an unexpected element? How? When? Where? Why?

• Ask for examples of previous solutions members have implemented and examine the obstacles they overcame.

4. *Problem*: There is some apprehension about the quality of the solution to be used in the plan of action. It is uncertain whether the solution will be accepted or capable of resolving the problem?

Possible solutions: • Use the criteria generated during solution-finding to help think of ways to strengthen and support the solution. • If solution quality appears to be high in spite of the group's fears, note that adjustments might be possible after implementation. Frequently, inaction is much worse than implementing what is perceived as an imperfect solution. Perfect solutions are not possible in most complex problem environments.

SUMMARY

CPS users and trainers should possess basic information on how to facilitate CPS groups. When designing training programs, guidelines such as the following may prove useful: hire an external consultant, gain broad-based support prior to implementing an internal program, create interest using trial programs that focus upon "fun" idea-finding techniques, and develop a cadre of internal facilitators.

The content of training programs can vary considerably. A short, half-day program might focus upon creative thinking skills and exercises. A longer program might include such exercises as warmup activities, but also describe the CPS stages in some detail. In addition, practice in the process and techniques should be provided using problems suggested by the participants.

Some general guidelines for facilitating CPS groups are: check to see that all equipment and supplies are available and ready when needed; use rooms that are adequate in size, lighting, temperature, and any other variables that might affect group process; establish ground rules prior to all sessions; to increase motivation, use practice problems suggested by group members; encourage "stretching" during divergence to generate as much information as possible; when presenting idea-finding methods, begin with those that rely upon related problem stimuli; model appropriate CPS behavior; be comfortable with short periods of silence; monitor time deadlines; encourage physical movement; check understanding using observed behavior, not verbal acknowledgements; maintain an informal atmosphere; practice effective listening methods; and encourage groups to strive for consensus during convergence.

When facilitating a group, different process problems are likely to arise. A number of responses are available for troubleshooting such problems. For instance, brainwriting methods can be used to overcome problems of interpersonal conflict or a dominating group member. Or, if a group has difficulty diverging during any stage, many idea-finding techniques can be used to help stimulate data.

Bibliography

Adams, J. L. (1979). *Conceptual Blockbusting: A Guide to Better Ideas* (2d ed.). New York: W. W. Norton.

Amabile, T. M. (1983). *The Social Psychology of Creativity*. New York: Springer-Verlag.

Borgstadt, C., & Glover, J. A. (1980). Contrasting novel and repetitive stimuli in creativity training. *Psychological Reports*, 46: 652.

Bouchard, T. J. Jr. (1972). Training, motivation, and personality as determinants of the effectiveness of brainstorming groups and individuals. *Journal of Applied Psychology*, 56: 324–331.

Callaway, M. R.; Marriott, R. G.; & Esser, J. K. (1985). Effects of dominance on group decision making: Toward a stress-reduction explanation of group-think. *Journal of Personality and Social Psychology*, 49: 949–952.

Carey, R. G. (1972) Correlates of satisfaction in the priesthood. *Administrative Science Quarterly*, 17: 185–195.

Coch, L., & French, J. (1948) Overcoming resistance to change. *Human Relations*, 1: 512–532.

Cotton, J. L. (1984). Why getting additional data often slows decision making—and what to do about it. *Management Review*, May: 56–61.

Covington, M. V. (1968). Promoting creative thinking in the classroom. *Journal of Experimental Education*, 37: 22–30.

Covington, M. V., & Crutchfield, R. S. (1965). Facilitation of creative problem solving. *Programmed Instruction*, 4: 3–5; 10.

Covington, M. V.; Crutchfield, R. S.; Davies, L.; & Olton, R. M. (1974). *The Productive Thinking Program: A Course in Learning to Think*. Columbus, OH: Merrill.

Crovitz, H. F. (1970). *Galton's Walk*. New York: Harper & Row.

Davis, M.; McKay, M.; & Eshelman, E. R. (1980). *The Relaxation & Stress Reduction Workbook*. Richmond, CA: New Harbinger Publications.

de Bono, E. (1970). *Lateral Thinking: Creativity Step by Step*. New York: Harper & Row.

Dewey, J. (1938). *Logic: The Structure of Inquiry*. New York: Holt.

Dominowski, R. L. (1981). Comment on "An examination of the alleged role of 'fixation' in the solution of several 'insight' problems" by Weisberg and Alba. *Journal of Experimental Psychology: General*, 110: 193–198.

Duncker, K. (1945). On problem solving. *Psychological Monographs*, 58 (5), Whole No. 270: 1–112.

Edwards, D. D. (1980). *How to Be More Creative*. San Francisco: Occasional Productions.

Einstein, A., & Infeld, L. (1938). *The Evolution of Physics*. New York: Simon and Schuster.

Etzioni, A. (1968). *The Active Society*. New York: Macmillan.

Feldhusen, J. F.; Speedie, S. M.; & Treffinger, D. J. (1971). The Purdue creative thinking program: Research and evaluation. *NSPI Journal*, 10: 5–9.

Geschka, H.; von Reibnitz, U.; & Storvik, K. (1981). *Idea Generation Methods: Creative Solutions to Business and Technical Problems*. Columbus, OH: Battelle Memorial Institute.

Getzels, J. W. (1975). Problem finding and the inventiveness of solutions. *Journal of Creative Behavior*, 9: 12–18.

Gilinsky, R. M. (1985). Meeting explores creative problem-solving. *New York Times* (Westchester County edition), November 24.

Glover, J. A. (1980). *Becoming a More Creative Person*, Englewood Cliffs, NJ: Prentice-Hall.

Grossman, S. (1985). Personal communication.

Grossman, S., & Catlin, K. (1985) Superheroes. Presentation at the 31st annual Creative Problem Solving Institute. Buffalo, NY: Creative Education Foundation.

Gryskiewicz, S. S., & Shields, J. T. (eds.)(1982). *Proceedings, Creativity Week IV, 1981* (105–139). Greensboro, NC: Center for Creative Leadership.

Guilford, J. P. (1950). Creativity. *American Psychologist*, 5: 444–454.

Guilford, J. P. (1959). Three faces of intellect. *American Psychologist*, 14: 469–479.

Hackman, J. R., & Morris, C. G. (1975). Group tasks, group interaction, and group performance effectiveness. In L. Berkowitz (ed.), *Advances in Experimental Social Psychology, Vol. 8* (pp. 45–99). New York: Academic Press.

Haefele, J. W. (1962). *Creativity and Innovation*. New York: Reinhold.

Isaksen, S. G., & Treffinger, D. J. (1985). *Creative Problem Solving: The Basic Course*, Buffalo, NY: Bearly Limited.

Janis, I. L. (1972). *Victims of Groupthink*. Boston: Houghton Mifflin.

Kepner, C. H., & Tregoe, B. B. (1965). *The Rational Manager*. New York: McGraw-Hill.

Kepner, C. H., & Tregoe, B. B. (1981). *The New Rational Manager*. Princeton, NJ: Kepner-Tregoe.

Kim, J. S., & Hammer, W. C. (1976). Effect of performance feedback and goal setting on productivity and satisfaction in an organizational setting. *Journal of Applied Psychology*, 61: 48–57.

Kolb, D. A.; Rubin, I. M.; & McIntyre, J. M. (1974). *Organizational Psychology: An Experiential Approach* (2d ed.). Englewood Cliffs, NJ: Prentice-Hall.

Latham, G. P., & Kinne, S. B. III (1974). Improving job performance through training in goal setting. *Journal of Applied Psychology*, 59: 187–191.

Latham, G. P., & Yukl, G. A. (1976). Effects of assigned and participative goal setting on performance and job satisfaction. *Journal of Applied Psychology*, 61: 166–171.

Lung, C-T., & Dominowski, R. L. (1985). Effects of strategy instructions and practice on nine-dot problem solving. *Journal of Experimental Psychology: Learning, Memory, and Cognition*. II (4): 804–811.

MacCrimmon, K. R., & Taylor, R. N. (1976). Decision making and problem solving. In M. D. Dunnette (ed.), *Handbook of Industrial and Organizational Psychology* (pp. 1397–1425). Chicago: Rand McNally.

MacKinnon, D. W. (1962). The nature and nurture of creative talent. *American Psychologist*, 17: 484–495.

MacKinnon, D. W. (1965). Personality and the realization of creative potential. *American Psychologist*, 20: 273–281.

McCaskey, M. B. (1982). *The Executive Challenge: Managing Change and Ambiguity*. Marshfield, MA: Pitman.

Maier, N. R. F. (1931). Reasoning in humans: II. The solution of a problem and its appearance in consciousness. *Journal of Comparative Psychology*, 12: 181–194.

Maier, N. R. F. (1963). *Problem Solving Discussions and Conferences: Leadership Methods and Skills*. New York: McGraw-Hill.

Maier, N. R. F. (1970). *Problem Solving and Creativity in Individuals and Groups*. Belmont, CA: Brooks/Cole.

Maltzman, I., Bogartz, W., and Berger, L. (1958). A procedure for increasing word association originality and its transfer effects. *Journal of Experimental Psychology*, 56: 392–398.

Mansfield, R. S.; Busse, T. V.; & Krepelka, E. J. (1978). The effectiveness of creativity training. *Review of Educational Research*, 48: 517–536.

Moder, J., & Phillips, C. R. (1970). *Project Management with CPM and PERT*. New York: Van Nostrand Reinhold.

Myers, I. B. (1980). *Introduction to Type*. Palo Alto, CA: Consulting Psychologists Press, 1980.

Olson, R. W. (1980). *The Art of Creative Thinking*. New York: Barnes & Noble.

Osborn, A. F. (1963). *Applied Imagination*. 3rd ed. New York: Charles Scribner's Sons.

Parnes, S. J. (1967). *Creative Behavior Guidebook*. New York: Charles Scribner's Sons.

Parnes, S. J. (1981). *The Magic of Your Mind*. Buffalo, NY: Creative Education Foundation, in association with Bearly Limited.

Parnes, S. J. (1985a). *A Facilitating Style of Leadership*. Buffalo, NY: Bearly Limited, in association with the Creative Education Foundation.

Parnes, S. J. (1985b). Workshop presented at the 31st Annual Creative Problem-Solving Institute. Buffalo, NY: Creative Education Foundation.

Parnes, S. J., & Brunelle, E. E. (1967). The literature of creativity (Part 1). *Journal of Creative Behavior*, 1: 52–109.

Parnes, S. J., & Noller, R. B. (1972a). Applied creativity: The creative studies project (Part 1). *Journal of Creative Behavior*, 6: 11–20.

Parnes, S. J., & Noller, R. B. (1972b). Applied creativity: The creative studies project (Part II). *Journal of Creative Behavior*, 6: 164–186.

Parnes, S. J.; Noller, R. B.; & Biondi, A. M. (eds.) (1977). *Guide to Creative Action*. New York: Charles Scribner's Sons.

Pearson, A. W. (1979). Communication, creativity, and commitment: A look at the collective notebook approach. In S. S. Gryskiewicz (ed.), *Proceedings of Creativity Week I, 1978*. Greensboro, NC: Center for Creative Leadership.

Perkins, D. N. (1981). *The Mind's Best Work*. Cambridge: Harvard University Press.

Pickens, J. F. (1985). Personal communication.

Raudsepp, E. & Hough, G. P., Jr. (1977). *Creative Growth Games*. New York: Jove.

Raudsepp, E. (1980). *More Creative Growth Games*. New York: Perigee.

Raudsepp, E. (1981) *How Creative Are You?* New York: Perigee.

Reitman, W. R. (1964). Heuristic decision procedures, open constraints, and the structure of ill-defined problems. In M. W. Shelly III & G. L. Bryan (eds.), *Human Judgments and Optimality* (pp. 282–315). New York: John Wiley.

Reitman, W. R. (1965). *Cognition and Thought*. New York: John Wiley.

Rose, L. H., & Lin, H-T. (1984). A Meta-analysis of long-term creativity training programs. *Journal of Creative Behavior*, 18: 11–22.

Rosenfeld, R. B. (1982). The development and philosophy of the Photographic Divisions' Office of Innovation (PDOI) system. In S. S. Gryskiewicz (ed.), *Proceedings of Creativity Week 4, 1981*. Greensboro, NC: Center for Creative Leadership.

Schaude, G. R. (1979). Methods of idea generation. In S. S. Gryskiewicz (ed.), *Proceedings of Creativity Week 1, 1978*. Greensboro, NC: Center for Creative Leadership.

Simon, H. A. (1973). The structure of ill-structured problems. *Artificial Intelligence*, 4: 181–201.

Stein, M. I. (1975). *Stimulating Creativity, Vol. 2: Group Procedures*. New York: Academic Press.

Stevens, J. O. (1971). *Awareness: Exploring, Experimenting, Experiencing*. Moab, UT: Real People Press.

Taylor, J. W. (1961). *How to Create Ideas*. Englewood Cliffs, NJ: Prentice-Hall.

Taylor, R. N. (1974). Nature of ill-structuredness: Implications for problem formulation and solution. *Decision Sciences*, 5: 632–643.

Thelen, H. A. (1972). *Education and the Human Quest* (2d ed.). Chicago: University of Chicago Press.

Torrance, E. P. (1962). *Guiding Creative Talent*. Englewood Cliffs, NJ: Prentice-Hall.

Torrance, E. P. (1963). *Education and the Creative Potential*. Minneapolis: University of Minnesota Press.

Torrance, E. P. (1972). Can we teach children to think creatively? *Journal of Creative Behavior*, 6: 114–143.

Torrance, E. P. (1974). *Torrance Tests of Creative Thinking*. Lexington, MA: Ginn/Xerox.

Treffinger, D. J.; Isaksen, S. G.; & Firestien, R. L. (eds.)(1983). *Handbook of Creative Learning*. Honeoye, NY: Center for Creative Learning.

Upton, A.; Samson, R. W.; & Farmer, A. D. (1978). *Creative Analysis* (rev. ed.). New York: E. P. Dutton.

VanGundy, A. B. (1981). *Techniques of Structured Problem Solving*. New York: Van Nostrand Reinhold.

VanGundy, A. B. (1982). *Training Your Creative Mind*. Englewood Cliffs, NJ: Prentice-Hall.

VanGundy, A. B. (1983). *108 Ways to Get a Bright Idea (and Increase Your Creative Potential)*. Englewood Cliffs, NJ: Prentice-Hall.

VanGundy, A. B. (1984). *Managing Group Creativity: A Modular Approach to Problem Solving*. New York: American Management Associations (AMACOM).

VanGundy, A. B. (1985). *The Product Improvement CheckList (PICL®)*. Point Pleasant, NJ: Point Publishing.

VanGundy, A. B. (1986). *Stalking the Wild Solution: A Problem-Finding Approach to Creative Problem Solving*. Buffalo, NY: Bearly Limited.

von Oech, R. (1982). *A Whack on the Side of the Head*. Menlo Park, CA: Creative Think.

Vroom, V. H., & Yetton, P. W. (1973). *Leadership and Decision Making*. Pittsburgh: University of Pittsburgh Press.

Warfield, J. N.; Geschka, H.; & Hamilton, R. (1975). *Methods of Idea Management*. Columbus, OH: Academy for Contemporary Problems.

Weisberg, R. W., & Alba, J. W. (1981). An examination of the alleged role of "fixation" in the solution of several "insight" problems. *Journal of Experimental Psychology: General*, 110: 169–192.

Wertheimer, M. (1959). *Productive Thinking* (enlarged ed.). New York: Harper & Row.

Whiting, C. S. (1958). *Creative Thinking*. New York: Reinhold.

Woods, M. F., & Davies, G. B. (1973). Potential problem analysis: A systematic approach to problem predictions and contingency planning—An aid to the smooth exploitation of research. *R & D Management*, 4: 25–32.

Index

About the Author

ARTHUR B. VANGUNDY is Associate Professor and Chairperson of Human Relations at the University of Oklahoma. He is the author of *Techniques of Structured Problem Solving, Training Your Creative Mind, 108 Ways to Get a Bright Idea, Managing Group Creativity: A Modular Approach to Problem Solving* and *Stalking the Wild Solution: A Problem Finding Approach to Creative Problem Solving*. He has conducted numerous workshops and training programs on creative thinking and creative problem solving techniques.